A GIRL FROM YAMHILL

BEVERLY CLEARY

A GIRL FROM YAMHILL

A Memoir

AVON BOOKS ◆ NEW YORK

The publisher and author gratefully acknowledge permission to reprint on page 110 lyrics from "Barney Google" © 1923 Warner Bros. Inc. (renewed). All rights reserved.

AVON BOOKS, INC.
10 East 53rd Street
New York, NY 10022.

Copyright © 1988 by Beverly Cleary
Published by arrangement with William Morrow and Company, Inc.
Library of Congress Catalog Card Number: 87-31554
ISBN: 0-380-72740-4
www.avonbooks.com

First Avon Books Trade Printing: February 1999
First Avon Camelot Printing: October 1996

AVON TRADEMARK REG. U.S. PAT. OFF. AND IN OTHER COUNTRIES, MARCA REGISTRADA, HECHO EN U.S.A.

Printed in the U.S.A.

10 11 12 13 OPM 15 14 13 12 11

Contents

PART ONE

Yamhill

Early Memories

Mother and I stand on the weathered and warped back steps looking up at my father, who sits, tall and handsome in work clothes, astride a chestnut horse. To one side lie the orchard and a path leading under the horse chestnut tree, past a black walnut and a peach-plum tree, to the privy. On the other side are the woodshed, the icehouse, and the cornfield, and beyond, a field of wheat. The horse obstructs my vision of the path to the barnyard, the pump house with its creaking windmill, the chicken coop, smokehouse, machine shed, and the big red barn, but I know they are there.

Mother holds a tin box that once contained George Washington tobacco and now holds my father's lunch. She hands it to him, and as he leans down to take it, she says, "I'll be so glad when this war is over and we can have some decent bread again."

My father rides off in the sunshine to oversee the Old Place, land once owned by one of my great-grandfathers. I wave, sad to see my father leave, if only for a day.

The morning is chilly. Mother and I wear sweaters as I follow her around the big old house. Suddenly bells begin to ring, the bells of Yamhill's three churches and the fire bell. Mother seizes my hand and begins to run, out of the house, down the steps, across the muddy barnyard toward the barn where my father is working. My short legs cannot keep up. I trip, stumble, and fall, tearing holes in the knees of my long brown cotton stockings, skinning my knees.

"You must never, never forget this day as long as you live," Mother tells me as Father comes running out of the barn to meet us.

Years later, I asked Mother what was so important about that day when all the bells in Yamhill rang, the day I was never to forget. She looked at me in astonishment and said, "Why, that was the end of the First World War." I was two years old at the time.

* * *

Thanksgiving. Relatives are coming to dinner. The oak pedestal table is stretched to its limit and covered with a silence cloth and white damask. The sight of that smooth, faintly patterned cloth fills me with longing. I find a bottle of blue ink, pour it out at one end of the table, and dip my hands into it. Pat-a-pat, pat-a-pat, all around the table I go, inking handprints on that smooth white cloth. I do not recall what happened when aunts, uncles, and cousins arrived. All I recall is my satisfaction in marking with ink on that white surface.

Winter. Rain beats endlessly against the south window of the kitchen. I am dressing beside the wood stove, the warmest place in the house. Father is eating oatmeal; Mother is frying bacon. When I am dressed, Father sends me to the sitting room to fetch something. I run through the cold dining room to the sitting room. What I see excites me and makes me indignant. Proud to be the bearer of astonishing news, I run back. "Daddy! There's a tree in the sitting room!"

I expect my father to spring from his chair, alarmed, and rush to the sitting room. Instead, my parents laugh. They explain about Christmas trees and decorations.

Oh. Is that all? A Christmas tree is interesting, but I am disappointed. A tree slipping into the house at night had appealed to me. I want my father to charge into the sitting room to save us all from the intruder.

Memories of life in Yamhill, Oregon, were beginning to cling to my mind like burs to my long cotton stockings. The three of us, Lloyd, Mable, and Beverly Bunn, lived—or "rattled around," as Mother put it—in the two-story house with a green mansard roof set on eighty acres of rolling farmland in the Willamette Valley. To the west, beyond the barn, we could see forest and the Coast Range. To the east, at the other end of a boardwalk, lay the main street, Maple, of Yamhill.

The big old house, once the home of my grandfather, John Marion Bunn, was the first fine house in Yamhill, with the second bathtub in Yamhill County. Mother said the house had thirteen rooms. I count eleven, but Mother sometimes exaggerated. Or perhaps she counted the bathroom, which was precisely what the word indicates—a room off the kitchen for taking a bath. Possibly she counted the pantry or an odd little room under the cupola. Some of these rooms were empty, others sparsely furnished. The house also had three porches and two balconies, one for sleeping under the stars on summer nights until the sky clouded over and rain fell.

The roof was tin. Raindrops, at first sounding

like big paws, pattered and then pounded, and hail crashed above the bedroom where I slept in an iron crib in the warmest spot upstairs, by the wall against the chimney from the wood range in the kitchen below.

In the morning I descended from the bedroom by sliding down the banister railing, which curved at the end to make a flat landing place just right for my bottom. At night I climbed the long flight of stairs alone, undressed in the dark because I could not reach the light, and went to bed. I was not afraid and did not know that other children were tucked in bed and kissed good night by parents not too tired to make an extra trip up a flight of stairs after a hard day's work.

When I think of my parents together, I see them beside this staircase. My big father is leaning on my little mother. Sweat pours from his usually ruddy face, now white with pain, as he holds one arm in the other.

I am horrified and fascinated, for I think one arm has fallen off inside his denim shirt.

He says, "I'm going to faint."

"No you're not." Mother is definite. "You're too big."

He does not faint. Somehow Mother boosts him along to the parlor couch. Later, after the doctor has gone, I learn that a sudden jerk on the reins by a team of horses has dislocated the arm, an accident that has happened before in his heavy farm work, for his shoulder sockets are too shallow for the weight of his muscles. Mother's determination always supports him to the couch.

Those Pioneer Ancestors

When I think of my father without my mother, I think of him sitting with his brothers after a family dinner. They are handsome, quiet men who strike matches, light their pipes, and as Mother said, "smoke at one another." When their pipes are puffing satisfactorily, one of them begins, "I remember our granddad used to say . . ."

I pay no attention, for I am "being nice" to my younger cousin Barbara. This is my duty at family dinners.

Father was the grandson of pioneers on both sides of his family. All through my childhood, whenever a task was difficult, my parents said, "Remember your pioneer ancestors." Life had not been easy for them; we should not expect life to be easy for us. If I cried when I fell down, Father said, "Buck up, kid. You'll pull through. Your pioneer ancestors did."

I came to resent those exemplary people who were, with one exception, a hardy bunch. My Great-grandmother Bunn was rarely mentioned. I pictured them all as old, grim, plodding eternally across the plains to Oregon. As a child, I simply stopped listening. In high school, I scoffed, "Ancestor worship." Unfortunately, no one pointed out that some of those ancestors were children. If they had, I might have pricked up my ears.

My Grandmother Bunn's parents, Jacob Hawn and his wife, Harriet, crossed the plains in 1843 in the first large wagon train to Oregon. Jacob Hawn, born in Genesee County, New York, in 1804, of German parentage, was a millwright, pioneering his life. His first wife, like so many pioneer women, died young. He then married Harriet Elizabeth Pierson. In 1834, when Jacob was thirty and Harriet sixteen, the couple left by covered wagon for outposts of civilization in need of mills for grain or lumber. In their covered wagon, they trundled to Wisconsin, Missouri, Texas, Louisiana, back to New York, and then continued on to Missouri once more. Four children were born along the way. On May 18, 1843, the family started for Oregon with a company of "three hundred souls all told . . . traveling by compass due West."

In her old age, Laura Aurilla, the eldest child, recorded her memories of that journey to Oregon with her family, "two yoke of oxen, two horses and a cow." She was eight years old. Her little brothers were six, three, and one month old. My great-grandmother was by then twenty-five.

Laura described the company as "a happy lot of people, all of one mind to go to the new country called Oregon." There was no sickness or fear of Indians, and in the beginning there was plenty of grass for cattle. Laura recorded that the prairie was black with buffalo. If an animal was killed, it was divided with every family and the hide saved for future use.

Laura wrote about the hazards of crossing the Platte River and of help from Indians, of bare country with buffalo chips the only fuel for cooking, and of trading with Indians for dried meat and salmon.

When food ran low, families camped off to themselves to prevent hungry children from teasing for what others might have. ("Never tease and never hint" was a pioneer rule handed down to me.) Everyone was relieved when they were able to buy flour at Fort Hall and to bathe and wash clothes at Soda Springs. The Nez Percé

11

Indians were good to the "Bostons," as Indians called the members of the wagon train.

Laura described the men cutting timber and clearing a road to cross the Rocky Mountains, and how her father "fixed up" the mill of Dr. Marcus Whitman, the missionary. When the wagon train reached the Columbia River in November, some travelers built rafts, while wagons and livestock were sent overland. Others, including the Hawns, bought canoes from Indians.

By November, Oregon was cold and rainy. The Columbia River and the Gorge, a funnel for raw winds, were full of rapids. Clothes were wet, the family hungry. When they were blown ashore, my great-grandfather built a fire and vowed to find food, "dead or alive." With a sharpened stick, he speared two salmon from a stream where the fish, "running upstream, were so thick their backs were out of the water." The family ate roast salmon "with no salt, pepper or bread" before they traveled on, walking around rough water and towing their canoe.

Laura recalled how hard they had to work to bail water out of the canoe, and how, on reaching Fort Vancouver, then a British settlement, at night, they nearly swamped the canoe. "Just then a man hailed us, 'Who comes there?' By this time Father was out of humer [sic], and told him it was none of his business."

The Hawns then learned that Dr. Whitman had sent an Indian ahead bearing the news that a millwright was on the way. The man, hired to hail everyone who came along, stood on a rock in the rain and cold for four days and nights waiting for Jacob Hawn, the millwright. "So our hardships were ended," Laura wrote.

With provisions supplied by Dr. John McLoughlin, the missionary, the family was taken to Oregon City, where millstones shipped around Cape Horn were waiting to grind the harvest into flour for arriving emigrants. Dr. McLoughlin put men to work building a house for the family while, under Jacob's supervision, others constructed the mill, the first in what would become, in 1859, the state of Oregon.

There is not a word of self-pity. Laura never refers to herself, only to "we." She was often tired, cold, and hungry, but so was everyone else. She must have taken responsibility for her little brothers, not easy when a foal, the first stallion in Oregon, was loaded into the wagon with the children. Hardship was to be expected when one was a pioneer. All her life she remembered that journey with wonder, and with pride at the part she had played in the history of the United States.

Jacob Hawn took up a plot of land near Oregon

City, later moving near Lafayette. He built grist mills and bridges in the Willamette Valley. He also built the Lafayette Hotel, sometimes called Hawn's Tavern, which was used for court sessions and religious services. It also became a schoolhouse, for Harriet provided a room for a school and room and board for a young man eager to teach. Jacob acted as postmaster while continuing to build grist and lumber mills. He died in 1860, at the age of fifty-six, of "the hemorrhage."

Harriet Hawn must have been a woman of strength and endurance. Before the death of her husband, she bore four more daughters, one of whom, Mary Edith Amine, was to become my grandmother.

Widowed, Harriet moved with her children to The Dalles, then a rough mining town, where she built a hotel. She lived in The Dalles until she died, apparently enjoying her hard life.

The Bunn side of my father's family was considered less interesting, the Johnny-come-latelies of the family, for Great-grandfather Frederick Bunn did not cross the plains until 1851. To the surprise of my generation, the Bunns are now better known than the Hawns because of the house in Yamhill, now an Oregon landmark.

Frederick Bunn was born in Murfreesboro, Tennessee, in 1825. He and his brothers and sisters were orphaned and divided among families

14

who could take an extra child. Frederick was reared by a Mr. Wright in Texas, but in 1851 returned to Missouri, where he married Elmira Noel. A wife was a valuable asset, for in 1850 the Donation Land Act had been changed to entitle a married man to twice as much land as a single man.

The couple set out for Oregon, a journey of great hardship for Great-grandmother Bunn. She became pregnant, and Indians, who had been friendly and helpful to the Hawns in 1843, had turned hostile by 1851. To be eighteen, pregnant, terrified, and living in discomfort and hardship was too much for the young woman to bear. Her only child, my grandfather, John Marion Bunn, was born in Carlton, Oregon, nine months after the beginning of the long, hard journey. Elmira became an invalid who lived in terror of Indians all her life, even though the Indians were often imaginary.

John Marion Bunn married Mary Edith Amine Hawn on September 30, 1872. They bought land in and around Yamhill and a wheelwright's house that they enlarged into the first fine house in Yamhill. They had ten children, eight of whom survived—five boys and three girls. The farmhouse at the time of my father's boyhood held three generations and was a lively place.

My father told one story of growing up in Yam-

15

hill. When he was fifteen, his father sent him to the butcher shop to buy some beefsteak. Instead of buying the meat, he continued, by what means I do not know, to eastern Oregon, where he worked on ranches all summer.

When I once asked my Grandmother Bunn if she had worried about my father when he did not return, she answered, "Oh my, no. We knew he would turn up sooner or later." Turn up he did, three months later.

All his father said was "Did you bring the beefsteak?"

The Little Schoolmarm

Many words are needed to describe my mother: small, pert, vivacious, talkative, fun-loving, excitable, easily fatigued, depressed, discouraged, determined. Her best features were her brown eyes; her shining black hair, which grew to a widow's peak on her forehead; her even white teeth; and her erect carriage. She had a round nose and a sallow complexion, both distressing to her, but she made up for these shortcomings with her sense of style.

Mother was born Mable Atlee in Dowagiac, Michigan, and became a classic figure of the westward emigration movement, the little schoolmarm from the East who stepped off a train in the West to teach school.

Her father, William Slater Atlee, arrived in the

17

United States from England in 1854, at the age of two, with his parents, Thomas and Jane, and a baby sister. The six weeks' voyage by sailing vessel with two infants was so terrible that Thomas and Jane, homesick for England all their lives, could never face the return trip.

Ancestors are often remembered for some small incident. Great-grandfather Atlee, a miller, is remembered as a man who read every spare moment and who carried a book wherever he went. He is also remembered for admiring the fly front of American trousers at a time when Englishmen wore trousers that buttoned on the sides. One day, equipping himself with buttons, scissors, needle, and thread, he went out into the orchard and clumsily remodeled his trousers, to the horror of his wife.

Great-grandmother Jane Slater Atlee is remembered as a jolly woman, a lively talker, who once was so busy chatting that she absentmindedly knit a sock with a foot two feet long for the small foot of her husband. She bore twelve children, five of whom survived.

Little is known of the family of my grandmother, Mary Frances Jarvis of Dowagiac, Michigan. Her father, Zeduck Jarvis, was well-to-do; she loved him, and all her life took pride in his having given the land for the local school. Her mother died of "the galloping consumption," and at the age of seventeen Mary Frances married my grandfather to escape her stepmother.

The marriage of William and Mary Frances produced three children: Guy, Henry, and Mable, my mother. In the beginning, the marriage of my grandparents, a poor young miller and the daughter of a prosperous landowner, must have been unhappy. Mother recalled that when she was a little girl, her father drank heavily. "There is nothing more terrible for a child than seeing her father carried home drunk," she often said. I believe her. However, my grandfather, after observing the deterioration of some of his drinking neighbors, concluded that no good ever came from liquor, and never drank again. Mother had a horror of any sort of alcohol.

Mother graduated from Dowagiac High School in 1903 after spending one unforgettable year living with an aunt and going to school in Chicago. She taught two years in Dowagiac, then emigrated west in 1905 to Quincy, Washington, with two cousins, Verna and Lora Evans, also teachers. They had been hired by mail to teach in what their teaching certificates called the "Common Schools of Washington."

One letter to her parents, written in round, upright penmanship, exists from this period of Mother's life. It comes from "School Marm's Hall." Mother's cousins had already begun teaching, and she was about to hire a livery to drive out to her school in Waterville, Washington, a school that she thought had about fifty pupils.

Her description of life in Quincy in 1905 is lively. All the bachelors and widowers had "taken to" the new girls in town. Word went around that the young women liked watermelon, and "the result was rather alarming. There are watermelons upon the floor, table and shelves, behind the doors and in the closet. We never venture upon the street, but what some designing fellow offers us one. We accept them all and do our best. . . ." The young teachers went to dances and took in "all the little one-horse shows going. We always tell everyone we are going, start early, walk slowly and never have to pay our own way in."

Mother saved from this period of her life a copy of *The Biography of a Grizzly*, by Ernest Thompson Seton, which had been sent by friends in Michigan. She told me that after she read the book aloud in Waterville, her pupils told their families about it. People began to come from miles around to borrow the book, which was read until its binding was frayed and its pages loosened, but Mother treasured it and in her old age wrote inside the cover in a shaky hand, "This book very soiled because it has been read by many many people, including boys and girls."

Mother was not the only member of the family

to come west. Her older brother, Guy, emigrated to Arizona, where he mined silver and turquoise. Back in Michigan, small-town water-driven mills were being replaced by large roller mills which, my grandfather insisted, milled "all the good" out of the grain, so he and my grandmother moved west and settled in Banks, Oregon, where they bought the general merchandise store and lived in six rooms above it. My grandmother turned one bedroom into a millinery shop, where she trimmed ladies' hats with style and an understanding of farmwives' financial problems.

The three young teachers spent their summers trailing through the West in their big hats and long skirts, traveling by train in coach cars, marveling at San Francisco the summer after the earthquake and fire, the sea through a glass-bottomed boat at Catalina Island, the pin that drops silently in the Mormon Tabernacle in Salt Lake City. Those years were perhaps the happiest in Mother's life.

Mother took a side trip to visit her parents in Banks. There, sitting on the steps of the store, was a tall, handsome young man wearing a white sweater and eating a pie, a whole pie. This man was Chester Lloyd Bunn. He and my mother were married on December 26, 1907, in Vancouver, Washington.

I have few clues to my parents' courtship.

When I asked about a pair of mandolins no one ever played, Mother laughed and said, "Before your father and I were married, we pictured ourselves sitting in a hammock strumming them together."

When I was about ten, I found, along with Mother's old *Teacher's Encyclopedia,* a composition book. I opened it and read aloud from her handwriting, "At last Lloyd came today."

Puzzled, I asked, "Why did you write that?"

Mother snatched the composition book from me and did not answer. It must have been the beginning of a diary kept while she was fulfilling her teaching contract in Washington and longing for the young man she loved. I don't really know.

The couple moved to Yamhill, where Lloyd, as he preferred to be called, was working the farm for the Bunn Farming Company, an attempt to hold together for the family the land left by their father, who had died, gored by a bull, the previous August.

The life of a farmer's wife came as a shock to my small, high-strung mother, ill equipped for long hours and heavy work. Three or four years later, Father saw that he was doing more than his share of the work on the farm, and the Bunn Farming Company was disbanded. My father's share of the farm, eighty-two acres, included the house and outbuildings. He was the only one of the five sons interested in farming.

On April 12, 1916, I was born in the nearest hospital, which was in McMinnville. Mother traveled there by train and lived in the hospital for a week while she awaited my birth. It was wartime, and there was a shortage of nurses, so she busied herself running the dust mop and helping around the hospital until I was born.

McMinnville was my birthplace, but home was Yamhill.

The Farm

An only child on a farm, I had freedom for self-amusement, for looking, smelling, examining, exploring. No one cared if I got dirty. My parents were much too hardworking to be concerned about a little dirt. At the end of the day, Mother simply had me climb into my enameled baby tub set in the kitchen sink and scrubbed me off. The tub in the bathroom was almost six feet long, too long for one small girl.

Sunny afternoons, I sat among the windfalls under an apple tree that bore cream-colored apples with pink cheeks, sniffing the sun-warmed fruit, taking one bite, throwing the rest of the apple away, and biting into another. The first bite of an apple tastes best, and our tree was bountiful. Juice flowed down my chin. Nobody cared.

One happy morning when our crop of Bing cherries was wormy, I dug into the juicy cherries for worms, which I dropped into the mouths of baby birds in a nest I had discovered in a wild rose bush. When I turned up covered with purple juice, Mother said. "What on earth have you been doing?" and went on with her canning and preserving of fruit for the winter.

I hunted for the abandoned nests of hens that refused to lay their eggs in the hen house. The eggs were almost always rotten, and throwing them made a great stink. Father, watching me, said, "Just throw them over there in that empty field," and went on his way to the barn.

Most fun of all was tripping chickens. Father had a long pole with a hook on the end for snaring hens when Mother planned a chicken dinner. I tripped them, one after another, tipping them into the weeds of the barnyard, leaving them clucking indignantly over their ruffled feathers, until Mother pointed out that I was unkind to the chickens. I did not see why. I often watched Father behead chickens with an ax, a very unkind way to treat a chicken. I sometimes did not understand Mother's logic. When no one was looking, I went right on tripping chickens.

Freedom was permitted because Father had taught me rules of safety which I was trusted to obey. One cold morning, I had come downstairs to dress in the kitchen by the warmth of the wood stove. The heat felt so good I held out my finger to touch the stove.

"If you touch the stove, you will burn yourself," Father told me.

Defiant, I touched the stove and howled in pain.

Mother, who was dishing up oatmeal, was shocked. "Lloyd, how could you? Why didn't you stop her?"

"She has to learn sometime" was all Father said. Neither parent offered any sympathy. I had to learn.

In good weather, I followed my father around the farm, listening while he explained his work and taught me the rules I must obey.

Never play in the grain bin; the grain could slide down and smother me.

Never walk behind the horses; they might be startled and kick.

If I played in the haymow, I must always play in the center; if I played near the edge, I might slide into a manger below and frighten a cow or a horse.

Never enter the pump house below the windmill alone; the floor above the tank was rotting, and I might fall through.

Never walk uphill behind a load of hay; the hay might slide off the wagon on top of me.

Never lean over the pigpen; if I fell into the pen, the pigs would hurt me.

Always shut and fasten gates to keep animals from getting into fields.

All these rules, when explained by Father, seemed sensible and interesting. I understood and never disobeyed, not once.

I walked beside Father while he plowed and watched the rumps of Pick and Lady, our plow horses, rise and fall in the sun as the blade of the plow laid back the brown earth, and the dogs, Old Bob and Scotty, trotted beside us. Father taught me the names of the flowers that hid the split-rail fence: Quaker bonnets, which some people called lupine; wild roses; Queen Anne's lace, which looked to me like crocheted doilies on long pale stems. He taught me to sing songs about "Polly Wolly Doodle" and "The Bowery."

When he drove to the pasture for firewood, I sat beside him on a wagon seat polished by three generations of overalls while he named trees: maple, elderberry, alder, and cedar. He taught me, not very successfully, to imitate the whistle of the bobwhite. He sometimes climbed down to pick a purple thistle and a twig, which he magically turned into a tiny parasol for me.

When Father milked the cows, I stood beside him, watching his strong hands pull and squeeze the udders, making milk *ching-ching* into the

27

bucket. My hands were not strong enough to bring down milk. Sometimes he squirted milk into the mouths of a waiting row of barn cats.

I stood on the fence, out of the way, to watch Father work with the threshing crew as the men caught in gunnysacks the golden stream of wheat from the threshing machine. In spring, I stood on the same fence to watch another crew shear sheep, run them through a vat of sheep dip, and release them, naked and bleating, while hungry lambs searched for their mothers.

Late sunny afternoons, Mother escaped the house, and I joined her on a walk to the pasture to bring home the cows. Old Bob, crouching low, nipping heels, was capable of bringing home the cows without us, but Mother was glad of the sunshine and freedom from endless chores. These walks, with the sound of cowbells tinkling in the woods by the river, and bobwhites, like fat little hens, calling their names, filled me with joy as I searched for flowers whose names Mother taught me: shy kitten's ears with grayish white, soft-haired pointed petals which grew flat to the ground and which I stroked, pretending they really were kitten's ears; buttercups and Johnny-jump-ups to be gathered by the handful; stalks of foxgloves with pink bell-shaped flowers which I picked and fitted over my fingers, pretending I was a fox wearing gloves; robin's eggs, speckled

28

and shaped like a broken eggshell, which had such a strong odor Mother tactfully placed my bouquet in a mason jar on the back porch "so they will look pretty when Daddy comes in."

If we cut across a field, I picked bachelor's buttons, which Mother said were also called French pinks. Once when Father's sweater needed buttons, I picked some blossoms and, with a darning needle and thread, sat under the dining room table, where I sewed the bachelor's buttons to my father's sweater in place of the missing buttons. Although he disliked those flowers because as a boy he had been forced to weed them from the fields, he wore the sweater, buttoned with flowers, until the blossoms withered, crumbled, and dropped away.

Mother's work in the kitchen was so tiresome we were glad of distractions that took us, running, from the house. One day Mother thought she heard an airplane. We tore out to look. Sure enough, two army planes were flying right over our farm. We stood among the clucking chickens, watching in awe, until the planes disappeared into the distance. "Mamma, I could see the aviators," I said, almost not believing what I had seen—men up in the air.

Another time, those same hens set up a great chorus of squawking. "A hawk! A hawk!" Mother cried. "Quick, Beverly!"

All three of us knew what to do. Mother and I ran to the barnyard; Father ran to the barn. While Mother scooped baby chickens into her apron, I caught them one at a time. They were just the right size for my hands. One by one, I chased, snatched, and carefully carried the cheeping balls of yellow fluff to their triangular coops, where I shoved them to safety. Overhead, the hawk circled.

Father appeared in the doorway of the barn with his shotgun, fired, fired again. The hawk tumbled, flopping to the ground, a heap of feathers. Our chicks were safe from the talons of the hawk, and I have never forgotten my wonder at the feel of life in those chicks, whose bodies were so tiny and fragile inside their fluff. Even though I ran with them, I was careful to protect them with my curved and dirty fingers.

Winter days belonged entirely to Mother and were spent in the kitchen, where it was warm. I stood at the window watching the weather, the ever-changing Oregon clouds that sometimes hung so low they hid the Coast Range, rain that slanted endlessly on the bleak brown fields, stubble stiff with frost, and, sometimes, a world made clean and white by snow.

Because we were lonely for companionship, Mother talked while she boiled clothes in a copper wash boiler, ironed, baked, or worked at her hated chore, washing and scalding the cream separator. She recited lines she must have learned from an elocution class in Chicago when she was a girl. "There it stands above the warehouse door"—dramatic pause, thump of the iron on the ironing board—"Scrooge and Marley." These words from Dickens's *Christmas Carol* to me were mysterious and filled with foreboding.

In spring, Mother shared Chaucer, as much as she could recall: "Whan that Aprille with his shoures soote the droghte of March hath perced to the roote . . ." I learned to imitate every word, every inflection.

Mother also told me everything she could recall about her childhood in Michigan—sleigh rides, sledding, gathering sap for maple syrup. The Oregon maples in our pasture were a disappointing lot when compared with Michigan maples that gave forth sweet sap to be boiled and poured on the snow to cool for children to eat. I longed for the deep snows of Michigan. If we had snow like Michigan's, I could coast down our hill, if I had a sled.

Never mind, I could find substitutes. I took the broom to the top of the stairs, laid it on the steps with the handle pointing down, sat on the bristles, and descended the steps with terrifying speed, bumping every step and screaming all the way.

"How on earth did you get such an idea in your head?" asked my weary mother as she ran to pick me up and wipe my tears.

At Christmas I was given an orange, a rare treat from the far-off land of California. I sniffed my orange, admired its color and its tiny pores, and placed it beside my bowl of oatmeal at the breakfast table, where I sat raised by two volumes of Mother's *Teacher's Encyclopedia.*

Father picked up my orange. "Did you know that the world is round, like an orange?" he asked. No, I did not. "It is," said Father. "If you started here"—pointing to the top of the orange—"and traveled in a straight line"—demonstrating with his finger—"you would travel back to where you started." Oh, My father scored my orange. I peeled and thoughtfully ate it.

I thought about that orange until spring, when wild forget-me-nots suddenly bloomed in one corner of our big field. The time had come. I crossed the barnyard, climbed a gate, walked down the hill, climbed another gate, and started off across the field, which was still too wet to plow. Mud clung to my shoes I plodded on and on, with my feet growing heavier with every step. I came to the fence that marked the boundary of our land and bravely prepared to climb it and plunge into foreign bushes.

My journey was interrupted by a shout. Father

came striding across the field in his rubber boots. "Just where in Sam Hill do you think you're going?" he demanded.

"Around the world, like you said."

Father chuckled and, carrying me under his arm, lugged me back to the house, where he set me on the back porch and explained the size of the world.

Mother looked at my shoes, now gobs of mud, and sighed. "Beverly, what will you think of next?" she asked.

More rain fell. I stood at the kitchen window whining, "When's it going to stop, Mamma, when's it going to stop?"

Mother, who was as tired of rain as I, and worn out from being shut in with a restless child, fed wood from the woodbox into the stove and answered, "In Michigan, people say that when you can see a patch of blue the size of a man's shirt, the rain will stop."

I stared and stared at the gray, shifting clouds, watching. And then, just as if we were in Michigan, the clouds parted and I could see a patch of blue the size of a man's shirt. "Mamma!" I cried. "It's going to stop raining! I can see blue like Daddy's shirt." The blue patch enlarged. An arc of colors appeared. "Look, Mamma! Come look!"

Mother left her work to see the miracle.

"A rainbow," she said, "Isn't it beautiful? They say there's a pot of gold at the end of every rainbow."

The fragile colors contrasted with the soggy earth and the leafless trees of the pasture. Gradually the rainbow faded and disappeared, along with the shirt-sized patch of blue. Rain fell. This was Oregon, not Michigan.

Real spring came at last. On Sunday, we walked through misty rain down the muddy road to the white church, where I attended Sunday school in the basement and learned that Jesus loved me, and Pharaoh's daughter rescued a little baby boy she found in a basket in the bullrushes. Then the children joined their parents upstairs for the hard part of church, the endless sermon. Hymnbooks had no pictures. Finally, when I thought I could not stand it one more minute, the sermon ended, and we were released into watery sunshine under a ragged sky. There, once more, was a rainbow that ended not far away, at a wild crab apple tree blooming by the side of the road. I ran down the steps, past the buggies and restless horses, past automobiles, and on down the road.

"Beverly!" Mother called out. "Where do you think you're going?"

"To get the pot of gold at the end of the rainbow." Silly Mamma. Couldn't she see the end of this rainbow was close enough to reach?

"Come back this minute," ordered Mother. Reluctantly I returned to face the affectionate laughter of the dispersing congregation. Mother explained that a pot of gold was something you read about in fairy tales.

In Yamhill we did not have fairy tales, but from bits of overheard adult conversation I was beginning to understand that gold was something like money, and money was needed to buy all we did not grow.

Mother's Rules

In addition to teaching me scraps of literature and the marvels of Michigan, Mother taught me rules. Her rules, if followed, would turn me into a little lady.

First of all, I must not swear. Just because Bob Perry, the town carpenter, swore did not mean I could. Harvest and sheep-shearing crews also swore but usually stopped when they saw me. I could not understand why. I loved to listen to them swear.

When we walked uptown on errands, Mother sprinkled her talk with rules, gently, more out of habit than any real desire to reprimand.

I must not swing on gates. I might break the hinges, and swinging on gates was not ladylike.

When we turned the corner by the Masonic

Hall, we stopped to exchange a few words with "Old" John A. Simmons. In Yamhill, "Old" was an honorary title, for many very old, hardy men and women were part of its population of about three hundred. Old John A., as everyone called him, was the town undertaker. Some keeper of vital statistics once wrote reprimanding Old John A. for not reporting Yamhill's deaths. He replied that he was doing the best he could, but no one in Yamhill had died that year. English daisies, like flat, pink buttons, grew in front of Old John A.'s house. Bored with the grown-ups' conversation, I started to pick some.

"Never pick other people's flowers," Mother said. "They don't belong to us." This was puzzling. Our farm was abloom with flowers, most of them wild, which anyone was free to pick. I longed to pick town flowers—Canterbury bells, peonies, delphiniums, and those little daisies.

We crossed Maple Street, the main street, to avoid walking in front of men who hung around the livery stable. This also was hard to understand, because I liked to watch the men spit arcs of tobacco juice, and to look inside at the hearse and the hack.

Crossing the street meant we got to pass the saloon with its swinging doors. I was curious about that saloon, which Mother so disapproved of, but Mother always seized me by the hand and pulled me along, chiding, "Never look under saloon doors. It isn't nice." I could not understand. Many daily activities on the farm could not be called "nice." Why was town different?

Safely past the livery stable, we crossed back over Maple Street. We usually met a relative or two. Sometimes it was Uncle Fred, my father's oldest brother, who had a fascinating bald head. After we passed him, Mother said, "You mustn't stare at Uncle Fred's bald head. You might hurt his feelings." How could I hurt his feelings when I so admired his bald head? I once tried to cut off my own hair so I could be bald, too.

We usually stopped at the drugstore for a few words with Uncle Ray, my one uncle who had been sent to college, because Grandfather Bunn felt he was too fat to ever become a farmer. My father had wanted to become a pharmacist, too, but his father said no, he was cut out to farm.

Uncle Ray generously handed an ice cream cone across the counter to his niece. "Say thank you and sit down to eat it so you won't spill" were Mother's rules.

"Thank you, Uncle Ray," I said before I sat at a round table at the back of the store near the mysterious little room filled with apothecary jars, beakers, and mortars and pestles where Uncle Ray mixed medicines. I licked my cone, swung my feet, and stared at Great grandfather Hawn's ox yoke that hung on the wall.

At Trullinger-Eustice, the general merchandise store, Mother made a small purchase or two, a spool of thread or a can of baking powder, and paused to chat with Lottie Allen, a saleswoman of strong opinions who pounded the dry goods counter with her fist and frequently said "absolutely, positively"—fascinating words.

As soon as we left the store, I began to sprinkle my conversation with the new words. "Little girls don't say 'absolutely, positively,'" said Mother, amused even as she made her new rule.

Sometimes we stopped at "Aunt" Fannie McKern's house. "Aunt" Fannie was not my aunt. The whole town, except Mother, called her Aunt Fannie. Mother said calling people not related to one Aunt or Grandma was a very small-town custom. I must call Aunt Fannie Mrs. McKern. "It's good manners."

Mrs. McKern fascinated all of Yamhill's children because she was "Central," which meant she operated the town's telephone switchboard from her living room. We loved to watch her plug cords carrying telephone calls into little holes that connected callers to the person called, and unplug them when the conversation ended. She also had a bearskin rug, which I admired. I got down on

39

the floor and lay nose to nose with the bear with his open mouth full of big teeth.

"Beverly, get up off the floor," said Mother. "We don't lie on other people's floors."

Mother dragged me past the barbershop, where I wanted to see whose face emerged from the lather the barber was scraping away with a straight-edge razor. Pressing my nose against the barbershop window, it turned out, was unlady-like.

We did, however, stop at the post office with its wall of little bronze boxes with dials that had to be turned a certain way before the box could be opened. Our box usually held *The Oregonian* and sometimes a magazine. In front of the post office, Mother, starved for grown-up conversation, paused to visit with other women. "Remember," she whispered, "little girls should be seen and not heard." This was one rule I loved.

Being seen and not heard, I gleaned all sorts of interesting information. A bride scraped burned toast on the back porch every morning; someone could hear it across a field. The ladies shook their heads and wondered what kind of meals *her* husband was eating. A woman had been heard to say, "I just love to knead bread. It cleans the hands so." The ladies clucked like hens and vowed they would never eat any of *her* bread. A minister's dog stole a neighbor's butter; someone suggested the minister had trained him to steal because the minister was going hungry in Yamhill. The ladies laughed, but Mother whispered to me, "They're just joking. They know he didn't train his dog to steal."

Sometimes the most interesting and mysterious conversations ended when Mother shot a glance at me and said, "Little pitchers have big ears." The ladies' sudden silence was insulting. I was not a pitcher, and I did not have big ears.

On the way home, we might meet Aunt Maud, my real aunt, who was famous for once riding a bicycle downhill over a cow lying in the road because she was too insecure to steer around it. Or "Grandma" Russell, who climbed up on her roof and repaired her shingles, even though she was well into her eighties. "That's a pioneer for you," Yamhill said. Or Quong Hop, who had come from China to build railroads and had stayed on. Now he owned a confectionery store and lived in a little house near us where I was never allowed to swing on the gate.

Sometimes we made a detour to pay a call on a very old man Mother said I must never forget. Why, Mamma?

"Because he is your Great-uncle Jasper, who crossed the Plains in a covered wagon when he was three years old."

41

Oh, was that all? I thought he was interesting because he always wore a white nightcap.

Everything and everybody in Yamhill was interesting. The trouble was I wanted to swear, peek under the saloon door, stare a bear in the eye, and swing on gates. I "absolutely, positively" wanted to do these things. Mother never seriously scolded on these outings and always returned refreshed and full of amusing stories for Father.

In addition to all her rules for deportment, Mother gave me guidelines for life. "Never be afraid," she often said.

So I was not afraid. When a cat had a fit and began to climb the wall, Mother did not know what to do. I plucked the animal off the wall, dumped it out the back door, and could not understand why Mother was first amazed at my courage and then frightened "half to death." The cat might have clawed or bit me. "But it didn't," I pointed out. Mother sighed.

When Father was going to slaughter a hog for our ham and bacon, Mother said I had better not watch. Naturally, this made me want to watch. As soon as Mother went out to the barnyard, I climbed the stairs to try to watch from an upstairs bedroom window. Because the window was too high, I pulled up a chair so I could look out. What I saw was much more interesting than a squealing hog. Below the mansard roof was a ledge about a foot wide, just right for me to walk on. I climbed out the window onto the ledge. Higher than the woodshed, almost as high as the horse chestnut tree, I began to walk around the house. I had not gone far before Mother saw me and came running until she stood directly below me. "Beverly!" she said quietly and urgently. "Stand perfectly still. Don't move." Then she shouted for my father.

Puzzled, I obeyed, as I always obeyed on the farm. Father also came running, saw me, disappeared into the house, and was heard taking the stairs two at a time before he leaned out the window. "Hang on to the shingles and back up slowly, one step at a time," he directed as Mother stood frozen beneath me. I couldn't see what all the to-do was about, but I did as he directed until Father reached out, grabbed me, and hauled me in through the window.

"What the Sam Hill did you think you were doing?" he demanded.

"Walking around the house," I said.

"Next time do it on the ground." Father never wasted words.

Mother, white and shaken, had rushed in to join us. "Beverly, you must never, never go out there again. You could have fallen and killed yourself."

"I wasn't going to fall," I said, and I was sure I wasn't.

One day we took the train to Salem, where Father was going to play his baritone horn in the Yamhill band at the state fair. The gentle tyrants, the cows my father loved so much, usually prevented us from going far from home.

I was not interested in the exhibits of farm animals, but I was interested in the Ferris wheel. Mother agreed to take me for a ride and paid for tickets; then we climbed into the gently swaying seat and fastened a bar across our waists to keep us from falling out. The wheels began to turn, and slowly we rose. Mother clutched the bar until her knuckles were white. When our rocking seat reached the top, the wheel's motor broke down and we were stranded. I had never been so high or seen such a view: neatly laid-out farms, automobiles crawling along roads, and in the distance, a train breathing out a plume of smoke. I wanted an even better view. I slipped out from behind the bar, happy and free, and stood up on the tilting seat. Mother gasped and grabbed my skirt. I held out my arms and made the seat tilt more.

"Beverly, sit down this minute," Mother said through clenched teeth.

"But, Mamma, I want to see." I was on top of the world and had only begun to look.

"Sit down!" Mother dragged at my skirt, forcing me to sit, spoiling my fun. I sat scowling until the Ferris wheel was repaired and we reached the bottom, where Mother demanded that we be let off.

I objected. "But, Mamma, our ride isn't over," I told her. "Nobody else is getting off."

Mother did not answer. She had to sit down awhile. When she recovered, she scolded me. "Don't you know you might have fallen?"

I could not understand why Mother was such a scaredy-cat. After all, she had taught me never to be afraid.

Children

Children were part of everything that went on in Yamhill. In winter we went to dances in the Masonic Hall, where, after sliding on the dance floor, we fell asleep on benches along the wall and were covered with coats. We sang or recited in church programs, and afterward ate drumsticks at potluck suppers.

On May Day, we took part in a pageant at the high school and ran around with bunches of wildflowers, which we left at people's doors. On Memorial Day, we went with our families to the old cemetery at Pike, where the graves of our pioneer ancestors were pointed out to us. We played among their tombstones while the adults weeded their graves. On the Fourth of July, we took part in a parade with little girls, dressed in their best, riding on the bed of a truck disguised with bunting as a float. I recall a man nailing a board across our stomachs so we couldn't fall off. Each girl wore a ribbon bearing the name of a state. I probably brought disgrace to Ohio as the only state whose white stockings had dirty knees.

School did not open until after the prune harvest, when the whole town turned out with picnic lunches to pick prunes to be hauled off to the dryer. Children played among the laden trees but were careful to stay away from the yellowjackets. I stayed away from them but loved to watch them suckling at the plump purple bosoms of fallen prunes.

I went to birthday parties where boys wore sailor suits and girls wore their best dresses, with big bows held to their hair by metal clasps. The curly-haired girls were lucky. Their bows stayed in place. We were always accompanied by our mothers, also dressed for the occasion. Sedately, we played London Bridge, drop-the-handkerchief, and ring-around-the-rosy. I could have played all day. Mothers chatted, and those with straight-haired daughters darted out to adjust slipping hair ribbons. Ice cream and cake were served, and we all went home.

Once I received a written invitation to come to play with Elma, the daughter of the town electrician. Elma had a little electric stove in which we baked, with the help of her mother, a little cake. The stove was plugged into a fascinating electric socket near the floor. All the houses I knew had one electric bulb hanging from the middle of the ceiling. After the cake was baked and the stove unplugged, Elma's father cautioned us that we must not touch the socket, which in those days did not have a built-in plug but had, instead, a tiny metal door. I could not keep my eyes off that door, which hid a round hole lined with metal the color of the sun. Finally, when no one was looking, I opened the door and stuck my finger in the hole. *Then* everyone looked, for I received a terrible electric shock, a shock that made me shriek. Everyone was nice about it, and Elma's mother comforted me, but I was ashamed. I did not mean to be naughty; I was only curious and did not think anyone would notice if I stuck my finger in just once.

My one companion was my cousin Winston; we were "practically twins" because we were born a month apart. But Winston, who took after my father's side of the family, was large, good-natured, and deliberate in thought and movement. I, who took after Mother's side of the family, was small, impetuous, and quick.

Sunday afternoons in winter, Winston sometimes came to our house to play in the sitting room, where Father always built a fire in the iron stove on cold Sundays when the house was surrounded by bare dripping trees, sodden earth, and endless rain. Mother read a magazine, and Father, in work clothes because he had to milk the cows, lay dozing on the floor behind the stove. He had so little time for rest.

One especially dreary Sunday, Winston and I were trying to amuse ourselves by drawing pictures on my blackboard. We were whining because we couldn't think of anything to draw.

"Why don't you see which of you can draw the best bird?" Mother thoughtlessly asked without looking up from her magazine.

I seized the chalk and quickly drew, near the top of the blackboard, several spread-eagled *M*'s, which to me looked like birds in flight.

Winston took the chalk and slowly and deliberately drew a fence below my birds. Then he carefully drew a bird perched on the fence. It was all there: head, wings, beak, eyes, and tail. I thought it was a silly bird. No bird had such big eyes.

To better admire his bird, Winston climbed up on a chair and sat with his legs sticking straight out in front of him. "My bird is better than your bird," he informed me.

"It is not!"

"Now, children," said Mother, perhaps regretting having pitted us against each other.

"Your birds are just scribbles in the sky," he said. The superiority of that boy!

"They are not!" I told him. "Mine are better than yours." No bird looked like Winston's bird, but birds in flight looked like mine, I thought. Anyone watching barn swallows wheeling and swooping would know.

"Mine's best." Winston, stolid and insistent, was not going to give in.

"It is *not!*" Before Winston knew what was happening to him, I grabbed him by the ankles and yanked him off the chair. He hit his head on the seat and began to howl. I knew instantly I had done a very bad thing.

"Beverly!" Mother was shocked.

Father sprang from the floor, seized me by my arm, and, with my feet scarcely touching the floor, yanked me through the cold dining room and deserted kitchen into the bathroom, where he sat down on the edge of the tub, turned me over his knee, and spanked me.

Now it was my turn to howl. "I'll be good, Daddy," I sobbed. "I'll be good!"

"By grab, you'll never do a thing like that again," he said, and left me shivering, weeping, sniveling, alone in the cold—but still unconvinced that Winston's bird was better than mine. I didn't care what anybody said. Mine were better. I knew they were. I also knew I deserved that

50

spanking, so I had no reason to complain about it or feel sorry for myself.

Eventually I came out of the bathroom and was made to tell Winston I was sorry. My feelings were hurt because Mother had already brushed and braided her long black hair. I always looked forward to doing this for her on Sunday evening.

Winston and I shared another experience, one which I enjoyed. I am not so sure about Winston. Because there was so little to do for amusement in small towns, a woman made a business of traveling around the Valley with a set of child-sized wedding clothes, staging Tom Thumb weddings. Mothers of boys and girls the clothes would fit were notified and assembled with their children in "Grandma" Bedwell's yard. I was dressed as the bride, Winston the groom. The long white dress with a veil and train seemed so beautiful to me. Winston's black cutaway jacket, long black trousers, white waistcoat, shirt with a stiff collar, and black bow tie were uncomfortable.

The taking of snapshots was the point of the whole event, and there we are, side by side, in my Baby Book, with Winston scowling; Winston scowling harder, seated on an apple box with Beverly's hand on his shoulder; Beverly seated on the apple box with Winston looking sulky, his hand on her shoulder; Beverly standing alone, hands clasped in front of her, eyes modestly lowered.

I longed to play, really play, with other children. A cousin, I somehow felt, did not count as "other children." One spring morning, when I expressed my wish, Mother told me the stork was going to bring me a new brother or sister to play with. For a farm child, I was remarkably naïve. I accepted her story about the stork without question because many of the birth announcements that came to our mailbox showed a picture of a stork carrying in its beak a baby suspended in a diaper.

"How will you tell if it's a boy or a girl?" I asked.

"Boy babies cry louder," Mother explained.

That afternoon, Winston came to play. Outdoors, under the lilac bushes, I told him my interesting new information about babies.

Winston had a sister, Donna—a nice enough kid but too little to count for much, I thought—so he knew more about these things than I. "That's not true," he said.

I was indignant. "It is so true. Mamma told me."

"It is not true," said Winston, surprisingly superior. He took down his pants and said, "There. See, that's how you tell a boy."

I was astonished and interested. Winston was right. Didn't Mother know about this? Somehow

I had a feeling she did but was hiding something from me.

I had no answer for Winston, so I merely said, "Oh." Then I lifted my skirt and pulled down my bloomers. Companionably, we pee-peed under the lilac bushes, adjusted our clothes, and never mentioned the matter again. And I never asked my mother another question about babies.

Years later, when I told Mother this story, she said, "My land, I had no idea anything like *that* was going on under the lilac bushes."

Grandpa and Grandma

When he was sixty-eight, my Grandfather Atlee decided to sell the store in Banks and retire to Yamhill. He and Frank, as he called my grandmother, had worked hard all their lives; they weren't getting any younger, and they had earned a rest.

I was sorry about the store, where I could help myself to gumdrops. Grandpa Atlee, a small, spry man with a bald head (but not as interesting as Uncle Fred's bald head) and a bushy moustache, always lifted me to the counter to sit with my legs dangling, happy and proud when he told his customers, "Yes, sir. She's the only granddaughter I got, and she's a crackerjack."

My grandparents packed up their belongings and moved into two of the upstairs bedrooms for the winter until they could find a house in Yamhill. I was glad to have them; so was Mother. That winter she escaped many of her farm chores to keep books for Yamhill's general merchandise store, where she was surrounded by people to talk to.

A gentle dumpling of a grandmother who worried about her tendency to "put on flesh," my grandmother sang Civil War songs she had learned in her childhood: "Tenting on the Old Camp Ground" and "John Brown's Body." I begged for a story. Her story was always the same:

> I'll tell you a story about Mother Morey.
> And now my story's begun.
> I'll tell you another
> About Jack and his brother.
> And now my story is done.

Grandma Atlee taught me to sew. My stitches were uneven, my seams crooked, but turning scraps of cloth into blocks for a doll's quilt gave me real satisfaction.

Grandfather took me on his knee and, using my fingers to count, taught me "arithmeticking." We progressed to adding and subtracting without fingers, and then to writing down the numbers on the backs of old envelopes.

In the spring, my grandparents moved to a house I could walk to alone, pausing at the door of the carpenter shop to say hello to Bob Perry and to watch him work with saws, hammers, chisels, and planes. At the blacksmith shop I stopped to watch the smith pump the bellows that made the coals on his hearth glow, then heat a horseshoe, bend it, and nail it to the hoof of a patient horse. Once, when he was not busy, he made me a ring from a horseshoe nail. At my grandparents' house, I paused to smell the warm red roses.

Most of all, I enjoyed time with my grandfather when he worked in his vegetable garden, which was full of wonder and beauty: fat pods of peas, new potatoes to gather when he turned the soil, brown lettuce and pale cucumbers that Grandma floated in a bowl of diluted vinegar with a bit of sugar, ruby-veined beets and feathery carrots to be harvested for winter, tomatoes to eat warm from the sun, green onions to eat with homemade bread, corn for people instead of cattle, string beans twining their way up tepees of sticks, small muskmelons the size of baseballs, round mottled watermelons, and strawberries. Wherever my grandfather lived, he grew strawberries.

Across the fence, Mrs. Roberts raised sunflowers for seeds to feed her noisy parrot. Grandpa explained that these plate-sized yellow flowers followed the course of the sun during the day. That was why they were called sunflowers. I often stood looking up at those heavy blossoms, watching to see if I could catch them following the sun. I could never stand still that long, but by evening there they were, facing the sun setting behind the Coast Range. I was determined to catch them the next day, but I never succeeded. I was too active. Grandpa sometimes paid me a nickel to sit still for five minutes.

One summer day, my grandfather took me on a mysterious journey. He wouldn't say why. We walked a mile to the train depot. Through the depot window we could hear the chittering telegraph sending and receiving messages over the humming wires strung along poles that stretched the wires far, far away.

"When's the train coming, Grandpa?" I asked, wild with excitement.

"Hold your horses," said Grandpa. "It'll come. Don't you worry."

At last the train could be heard, chuffing and tooting, and then seen, trailing smoke as it pulled into the station and waited, panting, until the conductor shouted "'Board!" and we were off on our mysterious journey.

In McMinnville, seven miles away, we joined a crowd headed for a big tent and found seats on narrow bleachers.

57

It was a dog and pony show: music, clowns, dogs in costumes walking on their hind legs, pretty ladies leading ponies in fancy trappings, all marching, dancing around and around a big wooden ring in the center of the tent.

I was dazzled. There was so much excitement, so much to see, I couldn't take it all in. My fingers grew sticky from Cracker Jack as I perched on the narrow board and tried to grasp every bit of this grand and lavish spectacle.

The best part of the whole show was a clown wearing great flapping shoes who led a fox terrier with a stubby tail. On the end of this dog's tail was an electric bulb, and then—the light was turned on! The little dog trotted happily around the ring with the light on the end of his tail flicking on and off, on and off. I laughed so hard my stomach hurt, and I couldn't wait to tell my parents about the wonderful sight I had seen in McMinnville.

That summer I walked back and forth between the farm and my grandparents' house almost every day. One day I asked if I could take off my shoes and stockings when I went to visit. "Yes," answered Mother, somewhat absentmindedly. "Don't step on any thistles, and come home in time for supper."

I dropped my shoes and stockings on the porch, wiggled my toes, and set off down the board sidewalk between the privet hedges, heavy with fragrance, to the road. The dust, which came up to my ankles, was as warm and as soft as feathers. I kicked up little clouds and was happy.

Then my feet began to grow warmer until I was uncomfortable. I didn't think of turning back. On a farm, no one ever gave up. No matter how we felt, livestock had to be cared for, fields plowed, crops sown, fruit and vegetables canned.

My feet became so hot I was in pain. I started to run, leaving a trail of dust behind me. As I ran past the blacksmith shop, I began to cry. The smith, a horse's foot between his thighs, stopped pounding on a horseshoe to stare. Asking for help from someone not a relative did not occur to me, any more than turning back, even though my feet felt as if they were burning. By now I was covered with dust. Tears streamed down my face, leaving muddy tracks. I began to shriek with pain, but there was nothing to do but run on. "Grandpa! Grandpa!" I screamed.

Finally my grandfather heard me and came running to see what was wrong. When he grasped what had happened, he plucked me out of the dust and carried me into the house, out of the sun. "Poor little young 'un," he said. "You poor little young 'un."

"Oh, you poor child," said my grandmother when she saw my red feet.

My grandfather sat me on a chair and fetched a pan of cold water for my feet. My grandmother washed mud and dust from my face before she hurried to make me a glass of lemonade. I sat with my feet in the pan of water, drinking lemonade and feeling much better. The house was cool, and I was surrounded by love. "There. That's the ticket," said Grandpa when I stopped crying.

That was the year Mother had said the stork was going to bring me a little brother or sister. Suddenly, one winter day, I was sent to my grandparents' house, with my nightgown, to spend the night—a real treat for me, because Grandma always read aloud from the newspaper the "Burgess Bedtime Story," all about Old Mother West Wind, Grandfather Frog, and rabbits that went lipperty-lop into the old brier patch. Grandpa let me look at colored pictures in his dictionary, pages of foreign flags and breeds of horses, cows, and dogs.

I stayed all the next day, even though Grandma had walked back to the farm. When she returned, she cooked Thanksgiving dinner, which she packed in a basket. Grandpa balanced the basket on his shoulder, and we walked the muddy road home. What fun, I thought, dinner arriving in a clothes basket.

At home, I was shocked to see Mother, pale

and with her black hair tumbled on the pillow, in the four-poster bed in the downstairs bedroom. I had never before seen Mother in bed in the daytime. She managed a weak smile and told me she had not been feeling well, but she could come to the dinner table.

Later that winter, when it occurred to me to ask when the stork was going to bring my little brother or sister, Mother merely said, "The stork changed its mind."

When I was an adult, Mother told me what had really happened. She had had a difficult miscarriage. Father, with the help of "Central," reached a doctor, who, after hours of anguish for my parents, arrived too drunk to be of any help. Furious, Father telephoned my Uncle Ray, who opened his pharmacy in the night and brought to the farm the medicine a sober doctor would have prescribed. He gave it to Mother illegally and, the next morning, forced the doctor to sign the prescription. No little brother or sister ever came to our house.

The Library

The summer I was five, farm life began to change. For the first time, the cookhouse did not come to our farm at harvesttime. No burly man with a wood stove built in a shack on a wagon bed cooked for our harvest crew. I did not get to hang around hoping, but never hinting, for a piece of pie.

Instead, Mother and Grandma Atlee cooked for the crew. All the leaves were added to the oak dining table; dishes of jam, chowchow, and pickled peaches were set out. The two women worked frantically, peeling, mashing, frying, baking on the big wood range in the hot kitchen, trying to prepare dinner before the crew began to complain of hunger. Finally they rang the dinner gong to summon the sweaty, dusty, sunburned men, who trooped across the barnyard to wash at the sink on the back porch and wipe their hands and faces on the roller towel.

As the men seated themselves, Mother and Grandma rushed in with platters of fried chicken, mountains of mashed potatoes, great bowls of green beans simmered with bacon for hours, piles of biscuits, coffee. More chicken, more string beans, biscuits, and coffee, followed by several kinds of pie.

One thresher fascinated me. He had no teeth and ate with his knife. I stood as close as I could get to him, watching him scoop up food with his knife, looking up at his mouth to see how he managed. The other men were amused; he did not seem to mind. Later, when I tried to eat with my knife, Mother explained that only men who were old-timers ate with knives.

Finally, when the men had eaten everything in sight, they returned to the threshing machine. I helped clear the table, and when Mother and Grandma began to wash dishes in water heated on the stove, Mother said, "Beverly, never, never, serve mashed potatoes to threshers. They disappear too fast." To her mother she said, "What will the men think of me, running out of potatoes like that?"

"Why didn't the cookhouse come?" I asked.

Mother sighed. "Because we simply don't have the money. Most farmers don't this year."

There were other hints that we did not have as much money as we would like to have. When the Chautauqua came to town, and men in suits gave what I considered boring lectures in a big tent, town children were excited about paying ten cents to drop a fishing line over a curtain and land a present. I was eager for my turn, but Mother whispered, "You mustn't ask. We don't have an extra ten cents." Even though I was heavy with disappointment as we left and trudged down the boardwalk toward the farm, I managed not to cry, because Mother was so distressed.

Then, one rainy afternoon, I was watching Mother try to retrim her hat when Father came in from the barn. "What are you building?" he asked, a clumsy attempt at a joke.

Mother burst into tears. "I just can't make it look like anything," she said, "and I don't know when I can ever afford a new hat." I cried, too, so much did I want Mother to like her hat.

As my parents grew downhearted, I grew increasingly restless. "Tell me a story, Mamma. Tell me a story," I begged, or whined, until Mother was worn out. She had told me over and over every story she could remember: "Little Red Riding Hood," "Three Little Pigs," "Chicken Little," "The Little Red Hen." She had recited every scrap of poetry she could recall. On Sundays my father read me "The Katzenjammer Kids" from the funny papers. Grandma Atlee continued to read the "Burgess Bedtime Story" from the newspaper, even though I never went to bed afterward.

My picture books were a book of Jell-O recipes that showed shimmering pastel desserts, and advertisements in *The Saturday Evening Post, The Ladies' Home Journal,* and *The Country Gentleman.* I looked for the fluffy yellow chick in the Bon Ami advertisement. "Hasn't scratched yet," Mother read when I asked her what the words said. The Dutch woman who carried a stick and chased herself around the can of Dutch Cleanser was a character I admired. To me, she stood for energy and hard work, two qualities necessary to livelihood on a farm. My favorite magazine characters were the Campbell Soup twins, chubby and happy, always playing together. I longed for someone to play with and wished I had a twin.

I owned two books: the Volland edition of *Mother Goose* and a linen book, *The Story of the Three Bears,* in which Mother Bear, returning from her walk, carried a beautiful bouquet of purple violets. Mother read both books until I had memorized them.

Mother, too, was starved for books, perhaps to take her mind off her worries. "Yamhill needs a library," she said. "There is entirely too much gossip. People would be better off reading books."

Somehow, in spite of all her work, Mother summoned energy to start a campaign for a library. The editor of the *Yamhill Record* cooperated by writing articles expressing the need for a county library "because there is no place in Yamhill where books can be obtained free," and explaining that "a county library would cost a man whose property was assessed at $5,000 only $1.50 a year."

Mother, too impatient for voters to raise their taxes, and probably suspecting they wouldn't, plunged ahead. She asked for donations of books and a bookcase or cupboard that could be locked. A glass china cupboard was carried upstairs to the Commercial Clubrooms over the Yamhill Bank. The community donated books, boring grown-up books with dull pictures that were a disappointment to me. Mother reported in the *Record,* "Little folks come in eager for a book and have to go home disappointed."

With this small beginning, Mother opened the library every Saturday afternoon, when country people came to town to shop and Uncle Ray put out in front of the drugstore his popcorn machine, where celluloid dolls bounced in the dancing popcorn. I looked forward to the walk uptown to the library, where, even if there were no books for children, I could sit in a leather chair with its stuffing coming out and be seen and not heard. I listened to talk with big words I did not understand, but I did understand when women spoke angrily about the high price of sugar and the cost of canning fruit and making jam when summer came.

Mother persisted. She arranged a silver tea to raise money for the library, and someone gave a luncheon at which a woman played a saxophone solo. The library now had sixteen dollars! Mother called a meeting for the purpose of securing a traveling state library for Yamhill. The *Record* reported, "Twelve ladies were present who made up in enthusiasm for a lack of numbers."

Mother wrote that the library had sixty-four permanent volumes, including Dickens, Scott, Eliot, and Hawthorne, and concluded her article with, "It is said that a young girl who reads George Eliot's *Adam Bede* will never give her parents much cause for worry." She also cautioned, "Let every person donating a book first ask himself if the book contains anything that might cause young people to form wrong ideas."

Next Mother reported that a hundred people

had asked for books. Men wanted adventure, a boy asked for forestry, an old lady who was ill sent in for cheerful stories, women who lived in lonely places asked for books. She concluded this article by saying, "Our children need and are entitled to the use of a library just as much as city children are."

Crates of books began to arrive from the Oregon State Library in Salem. At last Yamhill had books for children—and what good books they were! The first I recall was Joseph Jacobs's *More English Fairy Tales,* which included a gruesome little tale called "The Hobyahs." I was so attached to that story that Mother had to pry the book out of my fingers at bedtime.

Books by Beatrix Potter were among the many that came out of those state library crates. My favorite was *The Tailor of Gloucester,* not only because I loved the story, but because of the picture of the waistcoat so beautifully embroidered by mice. I studied that picture and knew that someday I wanted to sew beautifully, too.

Mother wearied of reading aloud so much. "I'll teach you to read," she said.

"No." I was firm about this. Little girls who were to enter the first grade in the fall had spent a day at school in the company of big girls. I had such a good time that I wanted to learn to read in the real school with other children, not in our kitchen alone with Mother. I could hardly wait.

That brave little library brightened the lives of many of us that winter, and in the spring, when flowers bloomed again, the library had a hundred and forty-two books in addition to sixty-two state books.

One Saturday was particularly pleasant because we combined picking flowers with walking to the library. Yamhill's war hero, George Welk, who had captured thirty-two Germans single-handedly ("I think he just got excited," said Mother), had written to the *Record* asking the people of Yamhill to collect blue pinks. The blossoms would be sent to Portland for sea color on the U.S. Marines float in the Rose Festival parade. "George Welk takes pride in knowing Yamhill can do it," wrote the editor. Mother and I, along with others, gathered armfuls of blue bachelor buttons, which we left in buckets of water in front of the store on our way to the library. This was the last time we picked wildflowers in Yamhill.

That summer everything changed. Father was proud of his bountiful harvest of heavy wheat, laden fruit trees, woolly sheep, fat hogs, cows that gave rich milk. This was followed by bitterness because he could not sell any of it for enough money to meet expenses. We stopped subscribing to *The Oregonian* because, as I understood it at the age of six when I missed "The Katzenjammer Kids," the *Oregonian* did not say nice things about farmers.

Someone had borrowed money, Father had agreed to cosign, and when the person (perhaps an uncle) could not repay, my father had to assume the debt. Years later, Mother recalled that year with sorrow. "We had everything," she said, "everything except money."

Money was needed for things we could not grow, that mysterious, invisible mortgage payment, a pretty hat.

One day Father, looking worried and exhausted, came in from the barn. "I've had enough," he said. "I'm quitting."

Mother, who had been standing at the kitchen stove, dropped into a chair. "Thank goodness," she said.

Father found someone to lease the farm, and our livestock was sold at auction from the wagon in the barnyard. When the animals were being led away, and Mother learned the amount of money they had brought, she said, "Oh dear." I was sad, without understanding why.

Our possessions were loaded onto a truck. We left behind the beautiful walnut wardrobe because, as Mother explained, city houses had closets. Then, with Grandma and Grandpa coming

70

along to wave goodbye, we walked to the depot to catch the train to a new life.

Leaving Yamhill did not distress me, for home was wherever my parents lived. I looked forward to Portland, where I would have children close by to play with, school, a real teacher who would teach me to read. Even though adults had troubles, I was secure. Yamhill had taught me that the world was a safe and beautiful place, where children were treated with kindness, patience, and tolerance. Everyone loved little girls. I was sure of that.

Mother worries because her daughter's ear sticks out.

ABOVE: Mother poses in her aunt's apartment the year she attended high school in Chicago. On rainy days on the farm she recalled this period of her life, particularly the opera, with longing.

RIGHT: Mother stands between her two cousins the year the three left Michigan to teach school in Washington. They find dressing in the clothes of a male relative hilarious.

Mother, in her high school graduation picture, faces the future with determination.

Father is photographed at the beginning of World War I for his mother, who insists on pictures of her five sons because they may go to war.

Mother and Father pose for their engagement picture.

My parents, at the time of their engagement, clown with Mother's cousin.

The entire farm is my playground, a sour of interest and delight.

My grandparents pose on the porch of the Bunn house in Yamhill.

I celebrate my first birthday by waving my very own hair-brush. Mother, who had tried to curl my hair, always re-marked of this picture, "I thought your hair never would grow in."

On my second birthday, when I have the measles, I refuse to hold still for the photographer. Swinging my legs was fun.

Winston and I stand together as bride and groom in the Tom Thumb wedding. I feel beautiful; Winston is miserable.

Winston and I are dressed for a party. By now my hair is thick enough to support a bow, even though the bow keeps slipping.

Too young to be trusted to wind the Maypole, Elma and I are bewildered flower girls in Yamhill's May Day festival.

Yamhill celebrates the Fourth of July by having a board nailed across the stomachs of little girls so they won't fall off the float. I represent Ohio, second from the left in the front row with dirty knees that show I have fallen down. The parade route is short because Yamhill's main street is only four blocks long.

Mother organized her library in the Commercial Clubrooms on the top floor of this bank building. Forty years later the china cabinet, empty of books, and the worn leather chair remained in the dusty room where a dead bird lay on the floor. (Yamhill County Historical Society.)

PART TWO

Portland

The Big City

Portland, city of regular paychecks, concrete sidewalks instead of boardwalks, parks with lawns and flower beds, streetcars instead of a hack from the livery stable, a library with a children's room that seemed as big as a Masonic hall, buildings so high a six-year-old almost fell over backward looking at the tops. I loved elevators that lifted me, leaving my stomach behind, and escalator stairs that moved, so I did not even have to raise my feet. Mother patiently rode up and down, up and down, with me.

On Halsey Street, we rented a six-room two-story house with a furnace instead of wood stoves; it seemed warm and cozy after the big farmhouse. The city lot had been part of a farm at one time, for old cherry and plum trees and a bramble of loganberries grew in the backyard. An acre or so of hazelnut brush flourished across the street, and beyond, in Sullivan's Gulch, railroad trains huffed and chuffed, dividing the city.

A plumber, who lived behind his corner shop, sang "O Sole Mio" into a washtub. A French widow, who took in boarders, lived next door. She had a fascinating accent and called me "Bev-airly." Best of all, children lived in almost every house.

And toys! I had never seen such toys. A boy who, with his father, boarded next door, had an Uncle Wiggily board game, Parcheesi, and Tin-kertoys. Girls had whole families of dolls. One girl, Elizabeth Ann, had a rocking horse, a tricy-cle, and, in the corner of her dining room, a large and completely furnished dollhouse. Her parents owned a radio, the first I had ever heard. Every-one had roller skates. I sat on the front steps, longing for skates of my own and for a skate key on a string around my neck, hoping someone would offer to lend me theirs.

And then one day my father brought home a pair of roller skates of my very own, and I, too, became part of the neighborhood, skating up and down the gentle slope. My knees were constantly skinned, but I picked myself up, screwed my skates in place, and skated on with blood trick-ling into my half socks. Sometimes I squatted on my skates and, with my arms wrapped around my legs, coasted down the slope.

We made stilts out of two-pound coffee cans and twine and clanked around the block yelling "Pieface!" at children on the next street and bloodying our knees when the twine broke. When we tired of clanking, or someone said, "For heaven's sake, children!" we pounded rose petals with rocks and soaked them in water, hoping to make perfume. We hunted for old bricks among the hazelnut bushes and pounded them into dust in a game we called Brick Factory. With scabs on my knees and brick dust in my hair, I was happy. I had children to play with who could be summoned by standing in front of their houses and yelling their names. Telephones were for grown-ups.

There was one problem, however, in the midst of all this joy. Because the children of pioneers considered education unnecessary for sons, who were expected to farm the land and hand it on to succeeding generations, my father's education consisted of two years of high school—all that Yamhill offered at that time—and a few courses in farming at Oregon Agricultural College, which left him ill equipped for city life. He became a night guard, from 7:00 P.M. to 7:00 A.M., for the Federal Reserve Bank, his one Portland connection. At some time in his youth, he had worked guarding Federal Reserve gold shipped by train to San Francisco. Trying to sleep daytimes with all the neighborhood children skating, yelling, clanking, and crying over skinned knees was difficult. He moved a cot to the attic and sometimes yelled out the window, "Quiet down there, you kids!" We tried to be quiet, until we forgot.

While my father slept in the attic, Mother took advantage of city culture and enrolled me in a ballet class overtown so I would become graceful. In Portland we did not go "uptown," as we had in Yamhill; streetcars took us "overtown" because we crossed the Willamette River. There, in a basement room (could it have been in the Civic Auditorium?), I laced my ballet slippers and shivered my way into a yellow camisole with attached bloomers, slipped my head through a hole in a square of yellow China silk, and tied a ribbon around my waist. With other shivering members of the class, including one resentful, tearful boy, we exercised at the bar under the direction of Alice May Brown and pranced around the room in steps with names that sounded to me like "gallop" and "sauté."

At home I galloped and sautéed around the living room while Mother played "The Glowworm" on our old upright Ludwig piano from the parlor in Yamhill. The neighborhood children, denied or spared this cultural activity, pressed their noses against the front window to watch. As her glow-worm glimmered around the living room, Mother said, "I do wish those children wouldn't smear the glass with their noses."

Mother also took me to the Portland Library Association, as the library was then called, where we walked across the marble floor, now hidden beneath composition flooring, to the room for children. Mother chose books to read aloud to me, and I ran my fingers along the spines of thousands of books I would soon be able to read to myself.

In the evening, Mother read aloud *The Blue Bird,* by Maurice Maeterlinck, the story of two children seeking the blue bird of happiness. "It's true," she said when she finished the book. "We find happiness in our own backyard." Mother did not have to tell me. Happiness was all around me. I couldn't wait for school to start. Then happiness would be complete.

School

Father brought home two books required for the first grade, *The Beacon Primer* and *The Beacon First Reader,* which cost fifty-two cents apiece. These businesslike books, with dark green covers lettered in black, were thin and easy to hold. I buried my face in the pages, inhaling the new-book smell, eager to join other children in reading from them.

The day after Labor Day, Mother walked me the six blocks to the two-story red brick Fernwood Grammar School, where I joined a confusion of children from the first through the eighth grades. Mother left me with other first-graders in the basement, where teachers lined us up, two by two. Clutching our books, tablets, and pencil boxes, we were all excited and bewildered.

Someone blew a whistle and called out, "Mark time!" Imitating other children, I pumped my knees up and down. "March!" Led by the first-grade teacher and still pumping our knees, we marched up the stairs to our classroom, where we were each assigned one of forty desks in five rows of eight, each row bolted to two boards so individual desks could not be moved. All the seats were occupied.

Except for one girl who lived across the street from me, the room seemed one big blur of children. Everything was strange: the American flag hanging indoors, the letters of the alphabet written across the top of the slate blackboard, the picture of a serene little girl in a white dress with a pink sash that hung above the blackboard.

The teacher was a tall, gray-haired woman who wore a navy blue dress and black oxfords. "Good morning, children," she said. "My name is Miss Falb. It is spelled *F-a-l-b*. The *l* is silent. Say, 'Good morning, Miss Falb.'"

"Good morning, Miss Fob," we chorused.

She then wrote *Miss Falb* in perfect cursive writing on the blackboard and instructed us to get out our tablets and copy what she had written.

The whole thing seemed unreasonable to me. If the *l* was silent, why was it there? I picked up my pencil with the hand closer to the pencil. Miss

Falb descended on me, removed the pencil from my left hand, and placed it in my other hand. "You must always hold your pencil in your right hand," she informed me.

No one had ever told me I had a right or wrong hand. I had always used the hand closer to the task. With her own pencil, Miss Falb wrote *Beverly Bunn* on my paper in the Wesco system of handwriting with its peculiar *e*'s, *r*'s, and *x*'s that were to become a nuisance all my life.

The business of right and left hands worried me all day. At home, I asked Mother how to tell one from the other. She happened to be sitting in front of the sewing machine, so she said, "Face the sewing machine." I did as she directed. "Your right hand is the hand closer to the wall." Oh. I went through the first grade mentally facing the sewing machine every time I picked up a pencil.

School always began with a strange song about "the dawnzer lee light." We sounded out words, *c-a-t* and *d-o-g,* and chanted rules: "*e* on the end makes *a* say *ā* in cake" and "*i* before *e,* except after *c.*"

Miss Falb passed out thin paper, about two inches square, for exercises in paper folding to teach us to follow directions. "Fold the paper in half," she directed. "Open it. Fold it in half the other way. Open it again. Fold each corner to the

98

center," and on and on. Mother marveled at my skill when I took my folded paper home.

Miss Falb supplied each of us with a small yellow box filled with blue cardboard counters the size of nickels. "Place five counters in a row," she directed. "Take away two. How many are left?" I liked the little counters, but, thanks to Grandpa, I could already add and subtract, and with real numbers, not counters—a skill Miss Falb did not notice.

Once a week we sang. Miss Falb taught us to stand, clutch our elbows, rock our arms as if we were holding imaginary babies, and after a *tweet* on her pitch pipe, sing something about "Baby's boat, the silver moon." Mother said it was a lovely song, but I preferred rousing hymns like "Bringing in the Sheaves" or "Yield Not to Temptation" any day.

At first, reading was dull but easy. The stories, though they could scarcely be called that, were about Ruth, John (What was that *h* doing in John?), and Rover. I managed "See mamma," "See kitty," and "I have a kitty." (Why were there two *m*'s and two *t*'s when one would do just as well?) Reading picked up after that, for gold stars were pasted on pages beginning "I have a doll," "I have a ball," and "Rover is my dog."

Then chicken pox kept me home from school for a week, perhaps longer, and ended my ballet lessons as well. When I returned to school, I had fallen behind. I got no more gold stars.

One day Miss Falb swooped down and whipped my hands with her frequently used weapon, a metal-tipped bamboo pointer. Probably this was for letting my mind wander, though I was not sure because I was so surprised. My hands burned, but I felt I must have been bad because at home I always knew any punishment was deserved. I tried to hide my tears of pain and humiliation and was too ashamed to tell my parents.

Miss Falb made children sit on a stool facing the corner. Once I was ordered, without being told why, to the cloakroom, where I huddled, sniffling, among rubbers and lunch bags. For weeks after that, the smell of peanut butter sandwiches made my stomach curl. Once a plump and cheerful girl named Claudine was punished by being sentenced to crouch in the dark cave under Miss Falb's desk with Miss Falb's feet in their ugly black oxfords. When her sentence was reprieved, she emerged chastened but not much worried. Claudine, a city girl all her life, was braver in class than I.

Soon every school day became a day of fear. When I needed to go to the toilet, I was afraid to ask to be excused because Miss Falb had scolded the class for asking to leave the room so often. I was also afraid to go alone down the steps to the girls' lavatory in the dim basement. One day, inevitably, I wet my pants. Miss Falb sent for the janitor to mop up my puddle and ordered me home to change my clothes. I walked six blocks with my wet bloomers *slish-slishing* with every step. Mother put me in fresh clothes and sent me back to school, where I was sure the whole class would remember my disgrace all the rest of their lives.

I began to beg to stay home from school.

"I'm surprised at you, Beverly," said Mother. "Show your spunk and remember your pioneer ancestors."

One day I enjoyed a treat. Donald, the boy who boarded next door, came down with chicken pox. Since I had already had chicken pox, I was sent to play with him. He was generous with his Tinkertoys, and even though he was older, he did not mind playing the Uncle Wiggily board game with me. I had a good time.

However, it soon developed that Donald had, not chicken pox, but smallpox. I, too, came down with smallpox. Even a fever and itching scabs were better than a day in Miss Falb's classroom.

Drama surrounded smallpox. The health department nailed a red quarantine sign to the front of the house. The milkman left milk on the bottom step and fled. My father was not allowed to live at home. He packed a suitcase and moved overtown to stay with his sister Minnie, who owned a small apartment house where any member of the family in need of help was welcome. For a treat, he had Meier & Frank's department store deliver delicious cookies topped with pink marshmallow cushions strewn with coconut. Mother read aloud *The Princess and the Goblin,* I ate those delicious cookies, and I did not have to go to school.

Mother thought my scabs would never drop off. In time, of course, the last scab fell away, the red sign was removed, and Mother lit the required fumigation candles throughout the house before she closed it up and took me overtown to the health inspector at the City Hall, who pronounced me fit for school. I did not realize how fortunate I was to be unpitted by scars.

Once more I was shoved out the door to go to school. By then I was hopelessly lost in reading. The class had been divided into three groups: Bluebirds, who found happiness in seats by the window; Redbirds, who sat in the middle seats; and Blackbirds, who sat by the blackboard, far from sunlight. I was not surprised to be a Blackbird.

The worst part of the day was the reading circle, where the Blackbirds in turn had to read words from the despised and meaningless word lists: "shad, shed, shod, shin, shun, shut, shot, ship, shop, shift, shell." We all feared and hated our turns at that circle of chairs in the front of the room as much as we dreaded trying to say the words on flash cards Miss Falb held up in front of the class. With luck, *party* or *mamma*, words I could read, were flashed at me. Oh, the relief!

From a country child who had never known fear, I became a city child consumed by fear. A three-year-old boy named Bobby, whose divorced mother lived across the street, came to stay with us for a few months while his mother was away looking for work. A disturbed little boy who wet his bed, Bobby needed the love and attention that Mother gave. I felt left out, as if Mother did not have enough love to go around.

An uppity Bluebird in the neighborhood made fun of me for naming my doll Fordson-Lafayette after a Yamhill neighbor's tractor and the town where Great-grandfather Hawn had settled. Dolls were supposed to have nice names like Alice or Betty. Nobody named a doll after a tractor. When children discovered I still believed in Santa Claus, everyone laughed at me. I had never endured ridicule in Yamhill. When I asked Mother about Santa Claus, she smiled and admitted there was no such being. How was I to know, alone on a farm where I believed so much that Mother told me? I did not mind disillusion in Santa Claus, but I felt that Mother had made me the butt of other children's derision.

Fear was intensified by adult talk of a terrible earthquake in Japan, where the earth shook, buildings crumbled, and thousands of people were killed. What if an earthquake happened in Portland? Suddenly I did not want my father to work nights. I wanted him home, safe, after dark.

And like the good little girl I struggled to be, I said my prayers at bedtime. "Now I lay me down to sleep. I pray the Lord my soul to keep. If I should die before I wake . . ." *If I should die before I wake.* The words suddenly were not just something I recited. They had meaning. I did not want to die like those poor people in Japan. If an earthquake came, I wanted Father there to save me. He could. I knew he could.

I lay in bed, determined to stay awake until he came home. I could not die if my father were home. I lay as flat and as still as I could so Death would overlook me, or a Thing hiding under the bed would not know I was there. I fought sleep, praying for dawn, for the first twitter of a bird.

I could not confess my terror. Mother had impressed upon me that I must never be afraid. If I told, she might love me even less than I felt she loved me since Bobby had come to live with us. When I did sleep, I frightened Mother by walking in my sleep down the stairs and out the front door. She said the sound of a sleep-walking child was the most ghostly she could imagine, and she began to sleep lightly, listening as she slept.

Meanwhile, at the bank, Father spent his nights quietly working with an unabridged dictionary on a contest to make the most words out of letters in a phrase I have now forgotten. He turned page after page of the big dictionary, writing thousands of words on tablets of paper, hours of labor that won him a Bee-Vac vacuum cleaner. He had expected a bigger prize—who else had such a big dictionary or such long nights for uninterrupted work? Mother said the Bee-Vac kept the rugs much cleaner than the carpet sweeper.

Between my fear of falling asleep, and not eating lunch, I must have looked peaked. Convinced that something must be wrong, Mother visited our class at school.

That day Miss Falb told Mother what a nice little girl I was and went out of her way to be kind. This confused me. When some of us were sent to the blackboard, I accidentally erased part of Miss Falb's example of writing that the boy next to me was supposed to copy. Fearing punishment in front of Mother, I began to cry.

"Why, Beverly, there's nothing to cry about,"

said Miss Falb, so gently I felt even more confused. This was not the Miss Falb I knew.

"Of course you didn't mean to erase the writing," she said, and rewrote the erased example while Mother, smiling, sat on a straight chair at the back of the room.

After Mother's school visit, life was worse than ever. "Please, Mamma, don't make me go to school," I begged. "Please, please!"

"Of course you have to go to school," she said. "Miss Falb is a very nice teacher. It's all in your imagination."

"It is not!" I screamed. "She's mean, and I hate her!"

"Now, show your gumption and remember your pioneer ancestors," ordered Mother as she shoved me out the door. I was fed up with all those pioneer ancestors, who only faced danger and starvation and did not have Miss Falb for a teacher.

Somehow the first grade came to an end. Free at last, I raced home with my report card.

Mother examined it and pointed out something I had overlooked in my escape, three words written in perfect script so pale it was almost invisible: "Passed on trial."

Mother looked sad. "Beverly," she said, "you must never, never tell anyone."

"Why?" I asked, unprepared for shame. The Bluebird who lived across the street had demanded to see my report card. She knew. I was filled with guilt.

"Because we don't want anyone to know," Mother told me; "and you must work harder in the second grade. If you don't, you might have to go back to Miss Falb."

I need not have worried about facing Miss Falb again. When school started in September, she no longer taught at Fernwood. She had been transferred to the open-air school for tubercular children.

Miss Marius

That summer, the children of the neighborhood skated once more. We skinned our knees tumbling off tin can stilts and played Lotto and Old Maid. Bobby's mother reclaimed her sad little boy, and Mother was mine again. Father began to work days instead of nights at the Federal Reserve Bank. I was now confident that I would live through the night, that no earthquake would turn our house into rubble, and no Thing lurked under my bed, ready to pounce if I moved. I forgot the ominous words "on trial," and entered the second grade refreshed.

Miss Tessie Marius, our second-grade teacher, was plump and blond, with a pink and white complexion. She was pretty, calm, gentle, kind and, in my memory, never wore navy blue. Miss

Marius, aware of my shameful record, asked me to come to her desk with my book, *The Beacon Second Reader*. She had me stand beside her, and there she quickly taught me to read—or perhaps I had already learned but had been frozen by fear.

The second reader was an improvement over my primer. There were no silly accounts of Ruth and John, Rover and Kitty, or stories of Tom and May going to the seashore. Seashore! No one in Oregon went to the "seashore." Oregonians went to the beach or "over to the coast." Everything in that primer had been pretty—brooks, books, dolls, doves, robins, ponies—and everyone happy—kissing papa, spinning tops, swinging high, and riding their stupid pretty ponies. *The Beacon Second Reader* had stories already familiar from Mother's library in Yamhill. "The Shoemaker and the Elves," "The Wolf and the Seven Kids," "Rumpelstiltskin"—all stories worth reading again.

Thanks to Miss Marius, I could read, but I refused to read outside of school.

"Everyone in our family has always loved to read," said my puzzled mother. "I can't understand why you won't."

Neither could I, but I felt reading should be confined to school, and only when required.

Miss Marius taught us a rousing song about a

peanut that sat on a railroad track with the train coming "a-chunk, a-chunk." When, in that last line, the train ran over the peanut, we all sang with glee at the top of our voices, "Toot-toot! Peanut butter!" Miss Marius also let us sing the popular songs of the day, "Last Night on the Back Porch" and a song about "Barney Google with his goo-goo-googley eyes." On Friday afternoons, before the last bell, we told jokes and riddles.

For exercise, we stood in the aisles, one hand on a desk, the other on the back of our seat, and recited, "Jack, be nimble. Jack, be quick." On "Jack jumped over the candlestick," we jumped over our seats.

In December, Miss Marius told us we could bring cake or cookies from home for a party the day before Christmas vacation.

Mother, however, was not to be persuaded. "My land, forty children, all with cakes and cookies!" she said. "Poor Miss Marius. You'll all get sick."

"But Miss Marius wants me to bring something," I insisted, for I knew a teacher's word was law to parents.

We reached a compromise. I took forty sticks of gum to pass out to the class, which turned out better than I had expected. The classroom was a mess, a glorious mess of crumbs, frosting, smeared faces, and sticky fingers. I walked up and down the aisles passing out welcome sticks of spearmint gum, which may have helped settle a few stomachs. No one threw up, at least not in the classroom.

Although the excesses of the party probably had nothing to do with it, I became ill with a sore throat and a high fever. Mother was frightened. She put me to bed on a couch in the dining room, where she could keep an eye on me. She piled on blankets, which I pushed back; she pulled them up again, saying, "You must stay covered up. You might get pneumonia." Mother was always afraid of my catching pneumonia or tuberculosis.

She consulted the Frenchwoman next door, who was a practical nurse. Mrs. Williams brought over a fever thermometer, which registered one hundred and six. She pulled off some of the blankets and advised Mother to call a doctor. He came two days later to say I had tonsillitis.

All I remember is a strange sinking sensation, as if I were going through a white tunnel toward a light at the end, with the sound of the telegraph wires of Yamhill humming in my ears.

I recovered to find my reader, delivered by a neighbor child, probably that Bluebird, on the couch beside me. At Mother's urging, but without enthusiasm, I picked up the book and read a story about American Indians. I felt a languid interest in the discovery that a reader could tell me something I did not already know. Then I laid the book aside.

The happy calm of the second grade was interrupted one day when Miss Marius asked us to stand and march into the third-grade classroom, where each of us had to share a seat with a third-grader. We discovered, propped up in the front of the room, a large black circle with numbers and letters painted on small white circles. Over this was another black circle, this one with round holes that revealed the letters and numbers underneath. We stopped whispering, giggling, and pushing to stare.

The third-grade teacher introduced a man from the telephone company, who explained that Portland was going to use the dial system. "All telephones must have dials," he said, pointing to the mysterious object in front of the room. The man explained the system of numbers and letters, moving the big black circle to show us how it worked. The top circle always returned to its original position after he moved it. The whole demonstration seemed so mysterious I did not understand it at all. His final words were "If you do not learn to use the dial system, *you cannot use the telephone.*"

I had never used a telephone in my life. In Yamhill I could not reach the wall telephone that

Mother cranked; in Portland there was a general understanding that telephones were for the use of adults. Children who wanted to communicate with their friends stood on the front porch and yelled their names until they came out. But now—where would we get one of those big black circles, where would we put it, and what if my mother and father did not know how to spin it to make it work? What if they didn't understand it any more than I did? They could never telephone Aunt Minnie or Grandmother Bunn. Father could never telephone home from work.

I ran home from school. "Mamma, Mamma," I cried, panting. "You can't use our telephone anymore! You won't know how. A man came to school and told us."

Mother laughed. "Oh, you're talking about the dial system," she said, and showed me the small dial on a new telephone and how it worked, remarking, "I do miss Mrs. McKern. She was always up on all the news in Yamhill." How easy! I wondered why the telephone man had made something simple seem so mysterious and difficult.

By the end of second grade I could read, although outside of school I flatly refused to open a book.

"Really, Beverly," Mother protested. "I simply

cannot understand what gets into you. You used to want to learn to read."

Neither did I understand what got into me, and I did not care. If Miss Marius was not around, nobody was going to catch me reading. I would do anything for Miss Marius. In her classroom, even in Oregon, the sun seemed always to shine.

The best day of all, that year in the second grade, was the day Miss Marius let me wash her little teapot after lunch. Then I knew for sure she loved me.

Gregory Heights

By the end of my second grade, Father changed to a new job: lobby officer in the new West Coast National Bank. He wore tailored business suits that hid his Smith & Wesson revolver in a shoulder holster. That he might ever have to use the Smith & Wesson never crossed my mind. In those days, Oregonians were much too well behaved to hold up a bank, at least, not often. At night the revolver, which I was told I must never touch, hung on the post of my parents' bed. I never touched it, not once, even though Father always removed the bullets and left them on the dresser.

After two years, the seven-room house we rented on Halsey Street no longer seemed small and cozy. The wood and coal furnace did not heat as efficiently as the wood stoves on the farm, and the open staircase at the end of the living room created a cold draft. Pipes froze. Mother was cold. She was also nervous about the trains, with hoboes in empty boxcars, that ran in Sullivan's Gulch. Children were no longer allowed to play in the hazelnut bushes between Halsey Street and the Gulch.

One night Mother heard, or thought she heard, someone pounding on the side door. The next morning dents were discovered, examined, discussed with the neighbors. Had they been there all the time, and we had never noticed? They looked fresh to some. Mother was sure she had heard someone whistle to an accomplice in the night. The story grew. There had been an answering whistle. Hoboes must have tried to break in. Mother decided it was time to move.

We rented a five-room house, with a glassed-in porch that served as a dining room, out on Seventy-seventh Street, a block and a half north of Klickitat Street—a neighborhood then five blocks from the city limit. Houses were far apart, and there were no children nearby. Hazelnut bushes, wild currants, and white marguerites grew in the rocky soil where garter snakes sunned themselves on warm days.

Mother was excited and a little frightened when we bought a gas stove with a thermostat on the oven. No more splitting kindling and struggling with dampers on the wood stove, or lighting a gas plate with a match. No more guessing at the temperature of the oven by the feel of heat on her hand. No more cakes that failed because of a wrong guess. Mother only hoped the whole thing would not explode.

The third-grade teacher at Gregory Heights Grammar School soon became ill and was replaced by a substitute who stayed the rest of the semester. Schoolwork was easy, but the substitute, I felt, could not be very bright. One day she asked a boy to make a sentence using the word "hot." He answered, "My pillow is hot."

"Don't be silly," she said. "Stoves are hot. Fires are hot. Pillows can't be hot."

Yes they can, I thought. I felt sorry for the little boy, who looked ashamed. Pillows could be very hot. Dumb teacher.

Mother discovered, in the basement of the Sunday School I attended, a glass case of children's books. The room was sometimes open evenings, so Mother and I walked to the church for books. She chose *The Princess and Curdie* to read to me, and two others, *The Dutch Twins* and *The Swiss Twins,* by Lucy Fitch Perkins, for me to read to myself. I had no intention of reading them. All I wanted to read were the titles of the silent movies at the nearby Roseway Theater. Movies were new to me, and exciting. I learned to read fast, before the titles disappeared from the screen.

The next Sunday afternoon was dreary. The outside world drizzled, the inside world was heavy with the smell of pot roast and my father's Sunday after-dinner cigar, and I was so bored I picked up *The Dutch Twins* to look at the pictures. Suddenly I was reading and enjoying what I read! It was a miracle. I was happy in a way I had not been happy since starting school. I read all afternoon until I had finished the book. Then I began *The Swiss Twins*. For once Mother postponed bedtime, until I finished the book.

Shortly after my discovery that grown-ups spoke the truth when they said reading was a pleasure, a newspaper club, the *Journal* Juniors, offered a free book to any child who would write a review. Mother suggested I do this, and I agreed. Mother took me, carsick all the way, over-town on a streetcar to the *Oregon Journal* building, where I was given a copy of *The Story of Dr. Dolittle,* a book I enjoyed even more than *The Dutch Twins*. When we returned with my review, a photographer took my picture, which was published along with the review. Suddenly I was a school celebrity. "There's that girl who got her picture in the paper," everyone said. No one mentioned reading the review.

Those two long trips to the *Journal* made me

dread streetcar rides, but I learned to endure them for the pleasure that lay ahead. To supplement our income, my father began to work Saturday nights as a bouncer at the Winter Garden Ballroom overtown. After supper, Mother and I sometimes took the long ride overtown, miserable for me because I had to fight carsickness, often with my face buried in my mother's lap, for seventy-seven blocks, over the bridge across the Willamette River, and into town. Not throwing up took willpower, all I could summon, as I gritted my teeth, clenched my fists, shut my eyes tight, and tried not to breathe the cold, stale streetcar smell until—just when I felt I must either die or disgrace myself—we arrived overtown. Mother bought the Sunday paper as we walked to the Winter Garden Ballroom.

I felt important when we were admitted free. We climbed the stairs to seats in the empty balcony, where I opened the paper and read the Sunday funnies on Saturday night—to me, a magical glimpse into the future. I knew on Saturday night the mischief the Katzenjammer Kids got into, while the rest of Portland had to wait until Sunday.

When I had finished the funnies, I leaned against the balcony railing, listening to the beat of the drums and banjo, watching the lights glimmer on the saxophone, trumpet, and trombone, following couples circling the floor, around and around, in the fox-trot, two-step, and hesitation waltz. My father paced the sidelines, keeping his eye on the dancers. Sometimes he stepped into the crowd, tapped a man on the shoulder, and spoke to him. I knew he had caught a glimpse of an illegal flask. The man and his partner always left quietly. Prohibition had been voted in since I had tried to peek under the saloon door in Yamhill.

Gradually the circling of the dancers made me drowsy; Mother pulled me back from the railing. Once again I laid my head in her lap, where, with the Sunday paper crackling above me as she turned the pages, I fell asleep. When I awoke, I was being carried over Father's shoulder from the streetcar to our house. How loved and safe I felt, the three of us alone, in the night, going toward home. I cherished those magic Saturday nights.

That year I fell in love, twice. At school I loved a boy named Johnny. During lunch period, after taking one bite out of my sandwich and sucking the juice out of my orange, I followed, or chased, Johnny around, much to his embarrassment, until the bell rang.

I also fell in love with the eighth-grade boy next door, who sometimes rode me to school on the handlebars of his bicycle, making me the envy of other third-grade girls. I loved him until the night our cat died. In the morning, Mother paid the boy to bury the cat in a vacant lot. Farm life had prepared me for the death of a cat, but the sight of a boy I loved carrying our cat by its tail outraged me, destroying my love. I wept in fury at this indignity to our pet.

That winter, freezing winds roared down the Columbia River Gorge, which was closer than we had realized when we rented the house. The glassed-in porch was too cold to use. Mother sparingly fed wood and coal into the furnace, trying to make it last the winter. Snow fell, melted, froze.

Mother bundled me up, pulling my knit cap down over my ears, wrapping a woolly scarf around my neck and over my nose, and pulling heavy stockings on over my shoes to prevent my slipping on ice. With her sweater held close around her, she opened the front door enough for me to slip through while she instructed me to walk in the middle of the street so I would not be struck by falling wires. In those days, bad weather was no excuse for closing schools or for keeping children home.

That solitary walk on icy streets was beautiful in a shining silver world under a cloudless sky of piercing blue. The only sound was the thud of ice-coated wires falling to the glazed crust of the snow. Sunlight transformed hazelnut bushes into

121

fairy-tale crystal; icicles were flashing daggers that plunged, stabbing the snow, before they shattered. The air was so clear and cold that breathing was painful, even through the layers of my woolly scarf. My nose ran, mittens did not warm my hands, but I was sorry to reach school, to leave the dazzling outdoors and enter the gray concrete building stuffy with the smell of little bodies and noisy after my radiant, silent walk.

By the time the snow had melted, our class had become 3B and had moved to another room and another teacher, a tall, pretty woman whose name, as I recall, was Mrs. Coad. She was a smiling, kindly teacher.

My only problem in 3B was the multiplication tables. In class we chanted in unison, "Two times two is four, two times three is six . . .," on and on.

"I don't hear you, Beverly," Mrs. Coad said, but she was nice about it.

The trouble was, we were expected to learn the tables all the way through the hard numbers, the sevens and nines. I absorbed the easy numbers by chanting, and tried to avoid being drilled by Mother on hard numbers.

One day Grandmother Bunn, who lived with her children in turn but spent most of her time with Aunt Minnie, came to stay with us. Mother had to go overtown in the afternoon, and that evening she planned a rare treat: taking me to the nearby Roseway Theater to see Milton Sills in *The Sea Hawk,* so Father could have a good visit with his mother. I was instructed to come straight home after school to keep my grandmother company.

Grandmother Bunn was tall, slender, and beautiful, with silver hair and flashing dark eyes. In her youth she had been famous, Mother said, and Father agreed, as the most beautiful woman in Oregon. She was kind and friendly toward me, but somehow I could never feel as close to her as I felt toward Grandma Atlee.

The prospect of an afternoon alone with Grandmother Bunn was daunting. What would we talk about? I disobeyed Mother. Instead of coming straight home from school, I went home with a girl in my class who lived about five blocks away; and when my conscience made me leave, Mother had returned home ahead of me.

"No *Sea Hawk* for you, young lady!" was her verdict.

I wept, I begged, I had to see *The Sea Hawk.* The whole school was going to see *The Sea Hawk.*

"Then why didn't you do as you were told?" Mother wanted to know.

I was sorry, I would be a better girl, I would never, never disobey again. My grandmother looked amused; Mother remained calm. I said I would *die* if I didn't get to see *The Sea Hawk.*

Finally Mother relented, but she exacted a price for my sin. Before I could go to the theater, I had to be able to recite, without mistakes, the multiplication tables, *including the twelves.*

"But that's not fair," I protested. "We aren't even up to the twelves in school."

"Suit yourself," said Mother, and went into the kitchen to prepare supper.

Cornered, I began the struggle. Grandmother Bunn, entertained by my dilemma, helped by listening to me recite. I learned fast. Mother and I left the house barely in time to catch the beginning of *The Sea Hawk.*

What a movie! That scene of a man swallowing a ring to keep it from the pirate, the pirate following him into the ship's cabin and emerging with a bloody knife in one hand and the bloody ring in the other. Gosh!—to use a word Mother forbade. That scene was the talk of the third grade on Monday, and I was secure in the knowledge that I knew my tables through the twelves when the rest of the class did not.

Mother did not care for *The Sea Hawk.* As an antidote, she took me overtown to see *Peter Pan,* with Mary Brian as Wendy and Betty Bronson as Peter Pan. I liked Captain Hook and the pirates, even though they were not bloody like the pirates in *The Sea Hawk.* I saved my ten-cents-a-week allowance for ten weeks so I could buy a copy of the book.

Gradually spring came to Seventy-seventh Street. Wild iris bloomed. One day a teacher came into the 3B room to announce that third-grade girls would take the part of lilac blossoms in the spring PTA program. She asked all the girls to stand. She then walked up and down the aisles, tapping girls on the shoulder. "The girls I have tapped will be lilac blossoms," she informed us, and left the room.

The teacher had not tapped me. One other girl had been skipped, but the rest of the girls had been cast as lilac blossoms. Never in my life had I been left out. In Yamhill, children were part of all that went on. At recess I waylaid Mrs. Coad to tell her I thought the teacher had made a mistake. Mrs. Coad kindly promised to speak to the teacher.

When the bell rang and Mrs. Coad returned, I was waiting with the other non-blossom. Our teacher told us gently that we had not been chosen because we were too short, but that we could be substitute lilac blossoms.

Too short! I did not feel short; I was tall enough for anything I wanted to do. Of course, in Yamhill I had been known as the Bunns' little daughter, but I thought this meant that adults were big and children little.

The lilac blossoms were all in remarkably good health. I watched sadly as they bustled off, full of importance, for rehearsals. At last a morning came when one blossom was absent. I eyed my rival substitute, who seemed unaware that anything unusual had occurred. The minutes dragged by until the recess bell. My seat was near the door, so I was able to dart out and down the hall. The blossom director was standing in a doorway talking to another teacher. I waited for her attention. Then, anxious to be fair to the other short girl, I said, "Excuse me, but one lilac blossom is absent today. Which substitute do you want to rehearse?"

The teacher put her hand on my shoulder, turned, and smiled at the other teacher. "This one," she said, "is a nuisance."

I stared at her in pain, while she looked amused, before I turned and fled, no longer wanting to rehearse, no longer wanting to be a lilac blossom at all. A nuisance, a *nuisance*—the word tormented me.

"What's the matter, Beverly?" Mother asked when I came home from school. "You look down in the mouth."

I shook my head, too ashamed to tell, because Mother might agree with that teacher. My parents believed teachers were always right.

The night of the program, I balked. "Of course

you're going," said Mother. "I have been elected president of next year's PTA."

"Can't Daddy stay home with me?" I pleaded. My father, I knew, did not like to go out in the evening. This time he wanted to go. I scowled and stuck out my lower lip.

"Get that look off your face," ordered my father.

"Beverly, I don't know what gets into you sometimes," said Mother with a sigh. "Now stop sulking and come along."

So, on that dreaded evening, all three of us walked to school and sat on folding chairs in the auditorium, with me in the middle, where I hunched down, trying to be invisible, a wretched, too-short nuisance.

"Sit up," ordered Mother, who was running out of patience. "Stop that slumping."

Reluctantly I raised myself an inch or two, while up on the stage the happy lilac blossoms rustled and twirled in their lavender and purple crepe paper costumes. I could scarcely bear to watch, and I never wanted to go to school again.

My Character and Music

Father tired of the long streetcar ride to work. Mother dreaded another winter of icy winds sweeping down the Columbia River Gorge. I did not say so, but I was fearful of having for my teacher the woman who thought I was a nuisance.

Mother resigned her upcoming PTA presidency, and early in the summer, we moved to tree-lined Hancock Street, half a block from Fernwood, my former school, which had sprouted two gymnasiums and an auditorium in the past year. Mother said I was just skin and bones, and now I could come home for a good lunch. She felt so cheerful about the advantages of the move for all of us that she went to a beauty shop and had her hair bobbed and permanent-waved. She came home smiling, with her long hair in a paper bag.

I now had a long walk to Sunday School while dreading having to read aloud a Bible verse with the word *womb,* a mysterious word, both in meaning and in pronunciation. However, the new Rose City Branch Library and the new Hollywood Theater were only a few blocks away.

Houses were close to one another, so close we could hear "The Prisoner's Song" or "The Song of the Volga Boatmen" played on Victrolas. All our neighbors had front and back lawns, and most had children the right age to play with. We played hard that summer: jump rope, hopscotch, and O'Leary with hard red rubber balls. Sometimes we did not play, but instead danced the Charleston, heels flying, hands crisscrossing between our knocking knees. If one of us fell down, the rest shouted "I faw down, go boom," a reference to a silly song about England's Prince of Wales falling off polo ponies.

"Good gracious," said Mother, "those children have all turned into flappers, and they're going right through the soles of their shoes."

Evenings when a comedy program was broadcast, neighbors with radios left their front doors open so children could settle like flocks of birds on their porches and listen. Some parent was always willing to take a few children to any civic event that might interest us. We saw Charles Lindbergh, blond and exhausted, paraded through Portland. We saw Queen Marie of Romania, holding a bouquet of purple flowers, ride down Sandy Boulevard. We saw the statue of Joan of Arc unveiled and were bored by speeches. And, of course, each year we sat on curbs to watch the Rose Festival parade.

We also went to the Hollywood Theater, an art-deco palace with Moorish towers above the box office. Inside, everything seemed red and gold. A Wurlitzer organ rose out of the floor by magic, with the organist already seated, ready to accompany the silent films.

Father took me to every movie with Lon Chaney or Douglas Fairbanks. My favorite was Douglas Fairbanks, who leaped from urn to urn in *The Thief of Baghdad* and slid down the sail of a ship by stabbing it with his dagger in *The Black Pirate.*

Mother preferred Mary Pickford or comedies. In *Sparrows,* Mary Pickford led a group of orphans across quicksand to save them from an evil man who was pursuing them, a scene so scary Mother found a piece of paper in her handbag for me to tear into little pieces so I wouldn't bite my nails until my fingers bled. When Harold Lloyd dangled from the hands of a clock far above a city street, children screamed with fright and excitement, and some of us were left with a permanent fear of heights.

Most of all, children hoped for an "Our Gang" comedy. To me, these comedies were about neighborhood children playing together, something I wanted to read about in books. I longed for books about the children of Hancock Street.

Worried about something I did not understand, Mother began to change. She decided it was time to mold my character. I was too old to call her Mamma. I was to call her Mother. Her rules followed me around the house like mosquitoes. "Use your head." "Stand on your own two feet." "Use your ingenuity." "Never borrow." "Use your imagination." And, of course, "Remember your pioneer ancestors," who used their heads, stood on their own two feet, always stuck to it, never borrowed.

If I lost something, Mother said, "You'll have to learn to look after your things." I did. If I was involved in a neighborhood squabble, I got no sympathy. "What did *you* do?" Mother always asked, leaving me with the feeling that, no matter what happened, I was to blame. "Try," Mother often said.

And try I did. When Abendroth's store across from Fernwood announced a contest sponsored by Keds shoes for the best essay about an animal, many of my class planned to enter. I chose the beaver, because Oregon was known as the Beaver State. On green scratch paper left over from printing checks, which Father brought home from the bank, I wrote my essay and took it to Mr. Abendroth. On the final day of the contest, I ran to the store to learn the results. I had won! Mr. Abendroth handed me two dollars. Then he told me no one else had entered the contest.

This incident was one of the most valuable lessons in writing I ever learned. Try! Others will talk about writing but may never get around to trying. I also wrote a letter to the *Shopping News,* which published the letter and paid me a dollar.

Fernwood was a relief after Gregory Heights. I had not been forgotten, nobody knew I was a nuisance, and my height did not matter. Johnny, my "love" from Gregory Heights, was there; his family had also moved.

Miss Pollock, our fourth-grade teacher, was a serious gray-haired woman who often reminded us that we should believe in "Gawd," apparently the same God I had learned about in Sunday School. She was kind and easily pleased. The fourth grade seemed to be one long quest for the lowest common denominator in long division. Sometimes I wished Miss Pollock's Gawd would help. For a treat, on Friday afternoons, we were allowed to recite poetry. I once recited "The Midnight Ride of Paul Revere" after being coached by Mother.

Once a week, we marched off to the music

room. Miss Johnson, the music teacher, always wore a green smock with a pocket that bulged with what we children suspected was a package of cigarettes but was probably a box of chalk. Miss Johnson was not a popular teacher, and I could never please her.

By the time I reached the music room, my stomach was a tight knot. We opened our songbooks and sang. Claudine, from the first grade, sat behind me, and when we began "If I were a student in Cadiz," Claudine sang "If I were a student in Hades." I admired and was cheered by her courage.

"Ring-ching-ching, ring-ching-ching, ring out *ye* bells," Miss Johnson enunciated distinctly. "Not ring *owchee* bells."

"Ring-ching-ching, ring-ching-ching, ring OW-CHEE bells," sang musical, carefree Claudine, spraying spit on the back of my neck.

We then had to take turns standing and singing alone. Please, God, let the period end, let the fire drill bell ring, let somebody throw up, before my turn. I sat, rigid, hoping the boy who had the courage to defy Miss Johnson would be called on first. His refusal to sing took up a lot of class time. He simply shook his head and sat mute. First his cheeks turned red, then his ears, while we sat fascinated by his defiance and by Miss Johnson's anger. The boy always won.

The music class made me so miserable, so sick with dread, that Mother gave up on my gumption and interceded. She went to school and explained my unhappiness over singing alone. On the next music day, Miss Johnson made another singing-dreader and me come to the front of the room and sing "America." We mumbled through, each trying to sing more softly than the other.

"Sing louder," ordered Miss Johnson. "Let me hear each word."

The girl and I exchanged glances of pure misery and mumbled more loudly on our second rendition of "America."

Fear of singing, however, did not stop me from wanting to be in the Christmas operetta, *The Cruise of the Trundle Bed,* about a little boy who fell asleep and dreamed he went to Toyland. I enlisted as a tin soldier because a short tin soldier was useful for leading marches, something I had to do almost every rainy gym period when we lined up according to height and marched in columns of two, four, eight; divided into fours, twos; marched single file in circles, on and on. Because I was the shortest girl in the class and always led the girls' column, I was good at marching, if not at singing.

On the night of the performance, dressed in blue and tan cambric soldier suits made by our mothers, we suffered one casualty, a girl who danced the Charleston on a chair and fell off, wounded, with a broken arm. Our troop regrouped and marched through our formations. When time came to face the audience and sing "The toyshop door is locked up tight. All the toys are quiet for the night," my courage left me. I mimed the words, a dodge noticed by my parents and every other parent in our neighborhood. "Why weren't you singing, Beverly?" they asked. "I didn't notice you singing." "What's the matter, cat got your tongue?" I thought they were rude, but I did not care. After my failure to be a lilac blossom, to be a fourth-grade tin soldier was a triumph, especially when a basketball, playing the part of a cannonball, was rolled across the stage and we all fell over with one leg in the air.

While school was often a happy place, sorrow was creeping into our home. Evenings, when my father came home from work, Mother's gentle greeting was always "Well, how did it go today?"

"All right." My father said little about his days at work, but then, he always was a quiet man. He could not have enjoyed standing eight hours on a marble floor, but he did not complain in front of me.

After supper, Mother still read aloud to my father and me. At first she read travel books and Greek or Norse myths, but more and more she searched for humorous stories, usually in *The*

Saturday Evening Post, which we bought for a nickel once a week from a neighborhood boy.

When I went to bed, I overheard worried, serious conversations. No matter how hard I tried, I could not hear what my parents were talking about. Finally Mother, desperate for a confidant, said to me in a voice filled with anguish, "Oh, I do pray your father won't decide to go back to the farm. For me, those years were years of slavery."

This was a complete surprise. Going back to the farm had never entered my mind. I had forgotten we still owned it. My father never mentioned in front of me his wish to return, for in those days parents did not discuss adult problems in front of children.

Tensions tightened. My father began to fly into rages over trivialities. A gentle man, he now terrified me by swearing, going into the bedroom, and slamming the door. I suffered over these outbreaks because I was afraid of what he might do when he came out. However, he always emerged quiet and in control of himself. Each time, I hoped such an outburst would be his last. I did not connect them with his dislike of the bank's marble floor or his longing to work outdoors once again.

Love and the Spelling Bee

Except for having mumps, I remember very little about the first half of fifth grade. I do recall that every day after lunch, we pulled out our composition books, and the teacher, a tense, unhappy woman, sat at her desk dictating numbers in sequence. We translated them into Roman numerals and wrote them down in columns. CLXXXIV, CLXXXV, CLXXXVI, CLXXXVII, CLXXXVIII, CLXIX. We had to think and write fast to keep up.

"Can't you slow down?" we objected. Our teacher ignored us. On and on she droned, her thoughts elsewhere.

Bored, lulled into drowsiness by her monotonous voice, most of us fell behind, skipped, and dropped out, only to begin again after lunch the next day. "Beverly comes home from school exhausted," Mother told the neighbors.

Miss Sampson, in 5B, was another teacher who wore navy blue and chalk dust and seemed old. She was kind but uninteresting. She gave us one homework assignment, the construction of a paper box the correct size to hold one gallon. Mine was wrong.

Johnny, the boy from Gregory Heights, now sat across the aisle from me. The class had decided, and I did not discourage them, that Johnny and I were in love.

One day Miss Sampson left the classroom for a few minutes. "Kiss her," someone whispered to Johnny. "Go ahead and kiss her!" The whole class began to hiss with insistence.

I was startled. Being in love was pleasant, but actually—kissing? What would Mother say if she heard about it? Johnny, interested, agreeable, daring, gave me a challenging look.

Accepting Johnny's silent dare, I extended the back of my right hand. Johnny took my fingers in his, as if he were a nobleman in a pirate movie, and kissed my hand, which I then quickly withdrew.

Miss Sampson returned, and the class immediately reassembled itself and tried to pretend it had been working on fractions the whole time. I sat blushing. A boy had kissed my hand! To this day, I have difficulty with fractions.

One morning I found in my desk a salmon-colored envelope. Inside was a matching sheet of paper with a downhill sentence printed in pencil: "I love you Bevererly." It was signed by Johnny. Happy that Johnny had finally, after three years, admitted loving me, I took it home to show Mother, who placed it in my Baby Book along with the record of my first tooth and first words. My first love letter is still there.

Acknowledged love was not the only change in my life. Mother found a piano teacher on the next street, and I began to take lessons, thumping away at scales and "The Happy Farmer" while Evelyn, an older girl who lived across the street, played rapid, accurate scales and "Rustle of Spring," probably counting out each note, on her baby grand piano. I felt hitting the right note should be enough without having to count at the same time.

After school, Mother would say, "Now I am going to have you practice," phrasing I deeply resented. Even more, I resented her sitting beside me, supervising my practice. However, music lessons had one advantage. Because I was so wretched over school music that I could not eat breakfast on music day, Mother arranged with the principal to let me take my piano lessons during music period. This kept me lackadaisically thumping.

When Grandmother Bunn came to visit, she listened to the frilly, trilly "Rustle of Spring" floating from across the street and offered me fifty dollars to learn to play it.

"No, thank you," I said politely, refusing to compromise my integrity.

That year a new girl appeared in the fifth grade, a girl who lived in the next block and who passed our house on the way to school. For the first time, I found a best friend.

Her name was Mary Dell. She had a sister seven or eight years old and parents who were younger than mine. Her father worked for a paint company. Mary Dell's mother seemed happy and carefree, often with a paintbrush in her hand, painting woodwork or kitchen cabinets. Once she even painted a pair of shoes. The family also kept a pet dog, a lively wire-haired terrier named Winnie. A dog in the house! On the farm we had two working dogs and a stray terrier that hung around, but none of them was ever allowed in the house.

Sometimes I spent the night with Mary Dell, and if my parents went to a party with friends from Yamhill who had moved to Portland, Mary Dell stayed with me. We did this until my parents gave up their modest social life. Long waits for streetcars at night spoiled their pleasure, and the serving of bootleg liquor at some parties disgusted Mother, who now felt she could no longer return hospitality.

I continued to spend the night with Mary Dell, whose mother did something I found surprising. She kissed her daughters. This filled me with longing.

I confronted Mother and informed her, "Some mothers kiss their little girls."

Mother laughed, pulled me to her, and gave me a hug and a kiss—a sweet, isolated moment. It was never repeated. I often look back on that kiss and wonder why Mother never felt she could kiss me again. She and my father often hugged each other, and my father was affectionate toward me.

One rainy day, Mother agreed that I could invite Mary Dell to our house to play. When I telephoned my invitation, I overheard Mary Dell speaking to her mother. "Beverly wants me to come over."

"Do you want to go?" her mother asked.

"Not especially," was Mary Dell's answer.

Shocked, I spoke into the telephone. "I heard what you said." I hung up, went to my room, closed the door, and cried. I cried because I understood Mary Dell's answer to her mother. My house was always cold and drab compared to Mary Dell's house; Mother was always tired and nervous. Why should Mary Dell want to come to my house? I understood perfectly, which made my distress even more difficult to bear.

The next morning on the way to school, I told Mary Dell, "I'm mad at you for what you said yesterday."

"What can I do to make up?" she asked.

Somehow I had not expected this reasonable answer.

"Get down on your knees and say you're sorry," I said.

To my horror, Mary Dell knelt on the sidewalk, placed her palms as if in prayer, and said, "I'm sorry." Then she rose, and we walked on to school as if nothing had happened. I cannot recall my reply, but I do recall the shame I felt (and still feel) over this incident that was so painful to me. There was no reason Mary Dell should have to be forgiven for a truthful answer to her mother. I wished my mother could be happier, more welcoming to my friends, who were almost never invited to our house.

A citywide spelling bee was announced. Mother was determined that I should enter. In school, when we took a spelling test, I slid through by somehow imprinting the words in my mind for a few minutes before they faded. If the test was given immediately, I spelled most of the words correctly.

The *Oregon Journal* printed whole pages of words in print so small I could not photograph them with my mind. Mother insisted I spell aloud as she pronounced each word. I stood on one foot and then the other, not wanting to spell at all.

"Stop wiggling," ordered Mother. I stared out the window; I scratched. Sullenly I spelled. Mother's lips compressed into a thin, straight line; my sighs of boredom and resentment grew more gusty.

When the preliminary spell-down was held in my classroom, I was given *beautiful*. "Beautiful. B-e-a-u," I began. Someone gasped, confusing me and making me feel I had made a mistake. I began again. "Beautiful. B-a-e-u—"

"Wrong," judged Miss Sampson. The class giggled. Everyone knew how to spell *beautiful*. So did I. Even though I felt silly, I was glad to be free of that city spelling bee.

Mother was so cross with me that I became angry. Without letting her know, I decided to do something bad, something really terrible. I decided to go a whole week without washing my face. That would show her, I thought, not exactly sure what would be shown, except a dirty face. Not washing my face that week gave me great satisfaction, except for one thing: no one noticed, not even Mother.

Mother bore down on me. "Don't sit on the edge

of the bed. You'll break down the edge of the mattress." "Sit up straight. You're growing round-shouldered." "Stop scuffing the toes of your shoes."

Clothes became the subject of the sort of argument Mother called a "battle royal." In winter she was adamant about two things: woolen underwear and high brown shoes that laced.

"No one at school wears woolen underwear or high brown shoes," I protested.

"You catch enough colds as it is," she said, "and no daughter of mine is going to grow up with thick ankles."

"Why don't you bind my feet while you're at it?" was my mean and sulky answer.

"Don't give me any of your back talk," Mother ordered.

"I don't care. I *hate* them," I cried, tears beginning to come. "I hate them, I hate them!"

No answer. Thin-lipped, unrelenting silence.

Every morning, sick with misery, I pulled on that short-legged, drop-seated woolen underwear, laced up those high brown shoes, and toyed with my breakfast in sullen silence before setting off for school, where, I was sure, everyone secretly laughed at my shoes. The underwear I was careful to keep hidden.

Adults, however, felt free to comment on my appearance, as if a child were unable to hear.

144

"Beverly looks more like her mother every day," they said, "but she's just skin and bones."

"Such big brown eyes," they said and canceled out my big brown eyes by adding, "but isn't it too bad her teeth are so crooked?"

Shoes and underwear worried me much more than my teeth, which were crooked, overlapping, and leaning in all directions. They were my teeth, and I was accustomed to them.

Toward spring I had tonsillitis again. In the night, once again the sensation of sinking downward through a white tunnel toward a light while the telegraph wires of Yamhill hummed in my brain.

"She looks like a ghost," the neighbors said, as if I could not hear. Why did adults think children had no feelings at all?

My parents were so worried about my health that Mother took me to a pediatrician—something almost unheard of in our neighborhood—who examined me, to my great embarrassment, and said I suffered from malnutrition and that I needed to get out and run on the beach. He also prescribed some sticky green medicine and told Mother to buy me some Scott's Emulsion, a tonic that made me gag.

When Father's vacation came, my parents dutifully packed a trunk with blankets, pots and pans, and new bathing suits for all of us; and we took the train to Rockaway, where we stayed in a one-room cottage equipped with beds, a table and chairs, and a wood stove. The pediatrician was unfamiliar with the Oregon coast, which can be cold and foggy in summer; or perhaps he did not expect to be taken literally.

Obediently I ran on the beach in spite of cold and fog, and like everyone who vacationed on the coast, we went into the Pacific Ocean every day—that was why we were there, wasn't it?—first consulting tide tables to make sure the tide was coming in so we would not be carried out to sea by undertow. Father enjoyed going out into the big breakers, but women and children jumped and squealed in small waves as we turned blue with cold and our teeth began to chatter.

The best part of that chilly vacation was raking crabs from tide pools and digging clams. I walked on wet sand, stamping my feet until a bubble appeared. As fast as he could move, Father cast aside a shovel or two of sand, knelt, and plunged his bare arms into the numbing grit to pull out a razor clam for chowder or fritters, which I refused to eat.

I am not sure this trip to the coast improved my health, but we all enjoyed it. The highlight for me was accompanying my parents to a dance. Because they felt I needed some sort of reward, they bribed me, quite unnecessarily, with a paper parasol to go along and behave myself. I was happy sitting under my open parasol on a bench, watching my parents have a good time fox-trotting to the music played by a small band. If only they would have fun more often . . .

Daytimes on the beach, I was instructed to stay away from the members of the dance band and what Mother referred to as "their women," who sat on blankets on the sand, passing around a flask. The women sometimes danced the Black Bottom while someone played a ukelele. Mother said I needn't watch. I peeked, and as soon as we returned to Portland, I showed the other girls how to dance the Black Bottom.

This journey for the improvement of my health took only two weeks, which left the rest of the summer. As in most of my grammar school summers, I passed the time sitting on the front porch, reading or embroidering. I embroidered smiling teakettles on potholders or knives chasing forks on tea towels until Mother bought a bedspread stamped with flowers to be worked in the lazy daisy stitch and big enough to keep me busy for a long time. My stitches never matched those of the mice in *The Tailor of Gloucester,* but I discovered how soothing handwork could be.

Awful Boys and a Decision

On warm evenings in the late summer of 1927, as children played statue or hide-and-seek, we caught scraps of adult conversation: "If interest rates go any higher . . ." "Wall Street." "The stock market." "Inflation."

Boring, grown-up talk, I thought, until one word, "inflation," came to have meaning for me. "It's terrible the way prices keep going up and up," said Mother. "Your father's paycheck doesn't stretch as far as it used to, and the worst of it is, the farmers aren't getting one cent out of it."

Because money would not stretch, Mother had our telephone converted to a private line. She set up the card table and, with the telephone book in front of her, began to solicit subscriptions to *McCall's* magazine, work she could do at home, so she would be there to prepare the lunch I barely touched, and again when I returned from school—the sixth grade in Miss Charlotte Stewart's room.

All the girls in my class seemed to have grown during the summer, but I remained the smallest. Most of the girls were nice, or tried to behave as if they were. By the sixth grade, many of us had caught on to the importance of pleasing the teacher, something I could do with part of my mind. This led to "Beverly, are you paying attention?" but did not really interfere with my being a nice girl.

The boys, who had not yet grown as much as the girls, had divided into two subspecies: quiet, serious boys and *awful* boys, feisty and rebellious, many of them swaggering because they had gone away to Boy Scout camp.

Miss Stewart's reputation, which had preceded her, proved accurate. Her favorite subjects were penmanship and spelling.

In penmanship, our pencils whispered around and around and back and forth on our papers while Miss Stewart walked up and down the aisles overseeing our work, repeating, "Sit up straight. Elbows on desks. Use your whole arm as you write."

We all worked at this dutifully, except for Ralph, a blond boy who sat across the aisle from me. Miss Stewart punished gum-chewers by making them stand in front of the class with their gum on the ends of their noses. Ralph modeled his gum into a small rhinoceros horn and faced the class with a defiant grin.

Ralph enjoyed teasing me. "Here comes Hot Cross Bunn," he said every morning.

"Pooh to you," I always answered.

With Ralph across the aisle, school was interesting. He once stirred up a little excitement by starting an *awful* boys' fad of eating garlic—a seasoning not widely used in our neighborhood at that time. Soon the room reeked of garlic. Girls held their noses and said "Ooh-eeh!" Boys grinned. Miss Stewart looked grim but said nothing.

Then one afternoon, Mr. Hugh Dorman, our principal, appeared. He ordered, by name, the garlic-eaters to stand. "March to my office," he commanded.

Girls murmured with delighted excitement, sure something terrible was going to happen to those awful boys, now looking so sheepish as they preceded Mr. Dorman to the office. We waited for them to come back chastened and contrite, but they did not. We exchanged puzzled looks. What could the principal have done with the boys? Would they never come back? Had they been expelled forever? We would not have admitted it, but we missed those boys who made the school-room lively.

The boys were not expelled. They returned the next morning, embarrassed and silent about their punishment.

Mother found out in that hotbed of information, the PTA. Mr. Dorman had gone across the street to Abendroth's store, bought a dollar's worth of garlic, and made the boys sit in his office and eat it all before he sent them home. A dollar bought a lot of garlic in those days.

About that time, a beautiful new girl moved into the neighborhood. I was eager to play with her to get away from the drone of Mother's voice soliciting magazine subscriptions. However, the girl's mother could be heard screaming at her family, none of whom ever smiled. Mother advised me to stay away. The girl and I eyed each other across the street, and at school we became bitter enemies. This was the first enemy I ever had. I felt sorry for her, and at the same time I genuinely admired her beauty and her fairy-tale hair. Probably she was hurt because I did not invite her to play, even though she was given a desk across the aisle from mine; perhaps she got back at me by making fun of my high shoes.

Miss Stewart now bore down on spelling. For each correct spelling test we were given one white star after our name on the blackboard. Five white stars were changed to one yellow star, five yellow stars to one pink star. After each spelling test—and we were tested frequently—we exchanged papers to be corrected by the person across the aisle.

My enemy and I exchanged, along with our papers, hostile looks that subtly changed into looks of collusion. No word was spoken, but somehow we had made a pact. We used our pencils, when we thought Miss Stewart was not looking, to correct each other's mistakes. I have no idea why we cheated for one another. Brought up to stand on my own two feet, I was contemptuous of cheaters and was now contemptuous of myself. Perhaps this was the beginning of adolescent rebellion, or perhaps beneath our hostility we were united by the tensions in our lives at home. Even though Miss Stewart surely must have been aware of what was going on, pink stars bloomed after our names. Perhaps she understood that the guilt those pink stars caused was enough.

At home, Mother grew hoarse and discouraged as she checked off names in the telephone book and recited her spiel about the stories of Gene Stratton Porter and Harold Bell Wright. When I came home from school that dark and dreary winter, I felt as if Mother, bundled up in an old sweater, had shut me out by endlessly repeating

152

the merits of *McCall's* to strangers over the phone.

To escape her weary voice, I went to Mary Dell's house or to a Camp Fire Girls' meeting; but most days I flapped in my galoshes to my haven, the red-brick Rose City Branch Library. The library had wicker furniture, plain parchment lampshades, blue-green shelves, and attractive paintings on the walls. It was warm, quiet, and peaceful. After finishing the mysteries by Augusta Seaman, I read over and over *Dandelion Cottage*, by Carroll Watson Rankin, because it was a humorous story about girls playing together. Like Mother, I sought funny stories about real people, but all the librarian produced was *The Peterkin Papers*, which I thought was silly. The adults I knew did not behave like the Peterkins, who seemed to me stupid rather than funny. I read my way through the shelves of fairy tales with their comfortable happy endings and started on Myths and Legends.

There I came upon the story of Persephone and her mother, Demeter. The flowers that enticed Persephone to stray from her companions reminded me of our pasture in Yamhill, where I had often been enticed to run on to a thicker clump of buttercups or a patch of fatter Johnny-jump-ups. In my imagination I became Persephone. Turning into the daughter of a Greek goddess was easy—I had had so much experience turning from a brown-haired girl with crooked teeth into a golden-haired or raven-haired princess in fairy tales. At home, the wet Oregon winter with its sodden leaves became the dark underworld, and somehow Mother's telephone soliciting kept the world from blooming. Demeter's search for Persephone comforted me. What would I have done without the library?

I read the beautiful myth over and over and each time found solace. I also came to understand that we cannot expect flowers to bloom continuously in life.

That winter, the dreaded tonsillitis again. My worried parents made a decision. My tonsils had to go.

As soon as I recovered, and the news of impending surgery spread around the sixth-grade classroom, Ralph rolled his eyes and made, with his forefinger, the throat-slitting gesture of a pirate.

"Pooh to you," I said, jaunty but apprehensive.

The dreaded day arrived. Mr. Brown, our former neighbor, offered to drive us to St. Vincent's Hospital on his way to work and bring us home in the evening as well.

The hospital was strange-smelling and awesome, with nuns in their mysterious long habits. An unsmiling nun assigned me a bed in the children's ward, a gloomy room with six beds. With shaking hands I undressed, put on the hospital gown, and climbed into bed. In the opposite bed, a frightened little girl was sobbing because this was the day her stitches from her appendectomy were to be removed, and she was sure it would hurt. Above her hung a picture of Jesus with a bleeding heart. The Jesus I knew sat with little children gathered at His knee, suffering them to come unto Him, or knelt at a rock with His hands clasped and a ray of light shining on His face.

"When it's over, you may have all the ice cream you want," Mother promised.

Terrified as I was, strapped to a gurney and wheeled down the hall, I fought to be brave. I would *not* cry. Outside surgery, my doctor paused to look down on me. "Well, well," he said, "and what are you here for?" If he didn't know, what was going to happen to me? Numb with terror, I could not answer. Inside surgery, something with a sickening smell was held over my nose, the world grew vague, and I sank into darkness.

I awoke fighting off blankets in the children's ward. My throat was raw. Mother stood beside the bed pulling up blankets as soon as I pushed them back. "Honey, you mustn't," she pleaded. "Please, honey, you must stay warm." *Honey.* Never in my life had Mother called me by an endearing name. In my groggy state, I wasn't sure I heard right.

"Sweetheart, you mustn't throw back the covers," she said. "You might catch pneumonia."

"Honey." "Sweetheart." Those words astonished me. Did they mean Mother loved me? Dizzy and confused, emerging from the dark underworld of anesthesia, I did not know what to think. Mother never said she loved me, and I must have felt that, sometime after we moved to Portland, she had stopped. Now—I was too groggy to think about such a puzzle. The room blurred. My tongue felt too thick to talk. Mother never called me by an affectionate name again. I have often wondered why.

As the day wore on and my mind cleared, I begged for water and the promised ice cream. Finally a nurse brought me a battered aluminum cup of orange juice, which felt like fire on my raw throat. Father had ice cream waiting when we returned home.

My health improved after the removal of the infected tonsils. Cheating in spelling ended by mutual, wordless agreement, and something unusual took place in the classroom. Miss Stewart read aloud *Smoky, the Cowhorse,* by Will James, winner of the *1927* Newbery Medal. The whole class, even Ralph, sat silent, engrossed. Here was a book about the West, written in language we had heard spoken in Oregon, that was not about noble pioneers. Anyone who had ever ridden a horse bragged. I had ridden behind my father when he rode a saddle horse on the farm, and on a pony rented for an hour at the beach—I felt I had much to brag about.

Ralph, with a jeering look on his freckled face, asked, "Do you know what a remuda is?" No. Well, he did. I was outbragged.

While life at school continued in its orderly way, stress at home increased slowly, like the jaws of a vise. My father's rages were more frequent. Mother said over and over, "I pray your father won't decide to go back to the farm. If only he would sell it."

I have never doubted my parents' love for each other, but I began to see they were locked into a problem they could not solve. My father could no longer bear to stand all day on a marble floor when he longed for an active life outdoors. Mother could not face the endless heavy work of a farmer's wife in the big cold house, or the long days of loneliness.

As Mother became more exhausted by the dreadful monotony of soliciting magazine subscriptions, she began to lose the beautiful black hair she was so proud of. First she discovered a small bare spot on the back of her head. Then other spots appeared and spread until a patch

157

the size of her hand was bald. She combed her hair back over the bald spot, wore a hat every time she stepped out of the house, and, frantic, visited a dermatologist. Yes, she would probably lose her hair, he told her, but she could always buy a wig.

Dad looked sad and worried, Mother was too distraught to continue telephone soliciting, and I was filled with almost unbearable anguish. Secretly, at night, I wept for my mother's hair.

Then one day Mother received a telephone call from a stranger, a friend of a neighbor, who had heard of Mother's plight. She, too, had once lost her hair, and told Mother of a home remedy that had saved it. The remedy sounded dangerous, and may have been, but Mother was willing to try anything. She obtained it, and my father applied a bit to a small spot on Mother's bare scalp to see what would happen. It was painful; a blister formed, and when the blister peeled away, as the stranger predicted, tiny black hairs were beginning to grow. Section by section, my father treated Mother's scalp, which gradually healed. Slowly, slowly, Mother's hair grew back.

My parents scraped up enough—or, as Mother said, "made sacrifices"—to send me for two weeks to Camp Namanu, run by the Camp Fire Girls. In the days before sleeping bags, I made my bedroll correctly, fastening it with blanket pins, and collected the required equipment. Dressed in a blue middy and black gym bloomers, I boarded a chartered train full of strange, singing girls also dressed in middies and gym bloomers. I was off for two weeks of fun. I knew, because I had read *Camp Ken-jockety,* by Ethel Hume Bennett, and series books passed around the neighborhood, in which children had happy times at camp.

For me, Camp Namanu, a beautiful place of woods and meadow, did not live up to camp in a book. Most of the campers had come in groups. Required swimming lessons in the cold Sandy River were misery. I did, however, earn the rank of Pollywog. The Namanu Honor, to be awarded to girls who were the best campers, was a worry. I strove to live up to mysterious, unspecified qualifications, but I failed, apparently a bad or perhaps unnoticed camper. I was not sorry to leave Camp Namanu, even though I enjoyed a dessert called Namanu Delight, a mixture of whipped cream and fruit. I felt guilty because Mother had sacrificed so I could have a good time.

When I returned, I learned Father had decided to sell the farm.

The House and the Car

Father found a buyer for the farm. Sixty-two acres of fields, an orchard, a pasture and woodlot bordered by the Yamhill River, a beautiful old house, and all the out-buildings brought $6,500. At some point earlier, Father had sold about twenty acres.

Father paid off the bank loan and a loan from Grandpa Atlee.

"Now at last we can afford a house of our own," said Mother.

"By grab, I'm going to buy a car," said Dad, "so we can get out of Portland once in a while."

"Of course," agreed Mother. "We all need to get out once in a while."

All I wanted was a sunburst pleated skirt, the kind that stood straight out when one twirled.

But Mother always hesitated to give me anything I really wanted. Because I was an only child, she was afraid I would become spoiled rotten.

"First things first," said Mother. "No daughter of mine is going to grow up with crooked teeth if I have anything to say about it." I was surprised. Other children wore bands on their teeth, but somehow it had never occurred to me that anything could be done about mine. I had accepted them.

With money in her handbag, Mother took me to an orthodontist named Dr. Meaney, a kindly man in spite of his name. Mother told Dr. Meaney she could not afford monthly payments, but offered him two hundred dollars to straighten my teeth.

Dr. Meaney examined my overlapping incisors and lopsided canines, considered the problem, and took me on, even though I was old to begin such extensive work. I have often wondered if he accepted out of kindness to a child, or if he did not often see two hundred dollars in cash when everyone felt pinched. My mouth was filled with warm wax, a mold was made of my teeth, and I was fitted with bands and wires.

For the next six years, I went overtown to his office, alone, twice a month, sometimes once a week. In his waiting room, where hundreds of plaster casts of crooked teeth grinned from glass cases, I saw some very interesting teeth but none as crooked as mine.

My father decided he could not wait his turn on the list of people eager to buy the new Model A Ford, which was replacing the Model T and which was so desirable because it was enclosed. Drivers would no longer have to climb out in the rain to snap on side curtains.

Dad bought instead a Model A Chevrolet with a black top and a dark green body so grand I stared in awe when it was delivered to our house. He got in and sat behind the steering wheel, where he began to study a book of directions. I climbed into the front seat beside him. With his eyes on the book and one hand on the ignition key, he started the car.

"Beverly, I think you'd better get out now," Mother called. With a few "damns," Dad taught himself to drive by reading each sentence carefully and following instructions—a sensible way to learn anything, I thought.

Every Sunday, Mother read real estate advertisements in the *Oregon Journal* and marked possibilities. Dad wanted a house with a porch where he could sit outside on summer evenings. Mother's requirements were a good neighborhood close to a good high school, solid construction, a location out of the wind, and plate-glass windows in the living room. I did not care where we lived.

With the marked advertisements in hand, we hunted the ideal house. To test the thickness of glass, Dad always produced a nickel, which he pressed against living room windows. The nickel cast a double reflection. The distance between the two reflections was the thickness of the glass. I always enjoyed the nickel test to see if the front windows measured up to Mother's expectations.

One house had a bedroom with a window seat where I could picture myself prettily leaning against cushions, reading a book like the girl in Jessie Wilcox Smith's 1924 Book Week poster. I sat on the window seat for practice and said that I liked this house. Mother frowned, shook her head, and whispered it was too expensive. I was not disappointed. All I really wanted, and desperately, was that sunburst pleated skirt. I became so bored with house hunting that I was finally allowed to stay home with a book.

In March of 1928, my parents found and bought a house that fulfilled their requirements, a square white house set on one of Portland's usual fifty-by-one-hundred-foot lots on Northeast Thirty-seventh Street, two blocks south of Klickitat Street and sheltered from the wind by a hill. We now lived one block from Claudine Klum's house, which was next door to that of the Miles family—parents and five daughters who had recently moved from Oklahoma, where Mr. Miles had sold his business and invested in the stock market. One of the girls, Lorraine, was a semester ahead of Claudine and me.

Our house had five rooms, a breakfast nook, a floored attic, and a half basement. Most interesting to me was a little door beside the back door, just big enough for the milkman to set two bottles inside so the milk would not freeze in winter or sour in summer. Whenever we locked ourselves out, I was boosted through the little door to unlock the back door from the inside.

I was given a choice of bedrooms and chose the front, even though I liked the back bedroom better. When friends came—someday maybe even boys—I wanted my parents separated from the living room by more than a wall. I was quiet about this thought. If Mother knew, or even guessed, I would have been given the back bedroom.

Mother made many trips overtown to choose curtains to harmonize with the elaborate wallpaper, which, if one studied the design closely, turned out to be exotic birds roosting on cauliflowers. She bought an overstuffed davenport and matching chair upholstered in scratchy taupe mohair, a covering popular at the time because it wouldn't show soil and would wear forever. Dad bought from his brothers and sisters several pieces of antique furniture that had furnished the

Yamhill house in his boyhood. He began to spend evenings refinishing them at a workbench in the basement.

Because I now had a longer walk to school, Dad bought me a secondhand bicycle. My Arizona uncle had sent me five dollars, which I spent on the sunburst pleated skirt in practical navy blue, the first new ready-made skirt I had ever owned. I enjoyed riding my bicycle in my sunburst pleated skirt past Ulysses S. Grant High School to Fernwood.

We were proud of the little white house with the porch box of geraniums and petunias and the green-and-white-striped awnings to shade the living room and dining room from the western sun that might rot our new overstuffed furniture. Mother gave a card party to show off our house to old friends who had once lived in Yamhill.

And then something frightening happened. On May 16, 1928, three months after we bought the house, a mortgage holder demanded his money. My parents were stunned. Inexperienced in buying property, they had not taken seriously the letter from their lawyer when they bought the house, pointing out that there was a mortgage against it "in the sum of $3,750.00 dated May 16, 1925, payable three years after that date." What would we do? We no longer owned the farm. All three of us felt numb.

Finally Dad, through the bank where he stood so patiently on the marble floor, was able to refinance the house, taking out a second mortgage, and we were saved—for the time being. Saved, but pinched for money once more. After that, whenever Mother left the house on an errand, she walked halfway to the corner and then returned—to make sure she had locked the back door, unplugged the electric iron, turned off the water heater—as if she was afraid the house might have disappeared when her back was turned.

With our house safe, we were now free to enjoy the car. First of all, we drove to Yamhill, where we parked at the foot of what had once been our path. Dad sat looking silently at his boyhood home, the home he had not seen since we moved to Portland.

"It really is a beautiful old place," said Mother with a sad smile. She could admire the house now that she was free forever from scalding the milk separator, cooking for harvest crews on a wood stove, and washing clothes on the cold back porch. To me, the house seemed almost as if I had read about it in a book, so many years—seven—had passed since we had lived there.

Next, as we drove around the small towns of the Willamette Valley, Dad appraised farmland with a practiced eye and pointed out property that had once been the Donation Land Claims owned by his aunts and uncles. Once we stopped to pick armfuls of fragrant wild trilliums, which grew in abundance in unfenced woods.

"See how each part of the plant is divided into threes: the leaves, the blossoms, the stamens, and even the pistil," said Mother, always the teacher. I marveled at the symmetry of the perfect blossoms of such intense sweet perfume.

Mother's interest in Oregon history was stimulated by our Sunday outings. "Just think—the names of these little towns tell how much this beautiful valley meant to the pioneers who braved the journey to get here," she said as we drove through Garden Home, Harmony, Sublimity, New Era, and Sweet Home.

In Oregon City, Mother pointed out the falls in the Willamette River where my Great-grandfather Hawn built the mill in 1843. As we drove up the Columbia River Highway, we stopped to admire every waterfall along the way. At Multnomah Falls, Mother reminded me that here my great-grandfather and his cold, starving family had been blown ashore during the dangerous trip down the river. My father and I climbed through the cave of brown, slippery rocks behind the falls, a thundering curtain of water between us and sunlight dousing us with spray while frogs leaped from our path.

We drove the narrow, twisting road to Mount Hood, where we stood above the timberline, but below the snow line, transfixed by the panorama of forest, of snow-covered peaks to the south, and of the Willamette Valley. "What a beautiful sight this must have been to pioneers after the long, hard journey across the Plains," said Mother in awe. "It really was the promised land." In the foreground near a pop stand, a caged bear drank Orange Crush from a pop bottle.

When Dad's vacation came, he wanted to return to the country he had run to when he was supposed to go to the meat market at the age of fifteen. He also wanted to visit his sister Dora, who lived near Prineville. Dad was concerned about her health because she had been ill with tick fever. We packed the Chevrolet with blankets and cooking utensils, which were not supplied by auto courts, and an army cot for me to sleep on and took off for two whole weeks of travel. At The Dalles, Mother reminded me that my Great-grandmother Hawn had built and run a hotel after the death of her husband and had survived both a flood and a terrible winter when horses froze standing up and Indians sliced off frozen flesh to thaw for food. Who cares, I thought, wishing Mother wouldn't go on so about Dad's grandparents. We turned south into scenery such as I had never known—and a country of sagebrush, juniper trees, and black lava rock. I had thought all of Oregon was as lush and green as the Willamette Valley, but of course I had never been a hundred miles from home before. We spent the nights in auto courts, where Mother always inspected the mattress for bedbugs, and Dad warned me to be on the lookout for rattlesnakes among the rocks.

Near Prineville, we turned off onto a dirt road so narrow that sagebrush clawed the car, bouncing over ruts and dipping through washes on our way to visit my beautiful Aunt Dora, the only female member of the family to resemble my grandmother. Aunt Dora taught in a one-room school someplace out in the brush. In good weather, older boys were kept out of school to work on ranches, so they continued in school long after city boys finished the eighth grade. When they did come to school, they were sometimes drunk. Dad felt his sister, weakened by illness, was working too hard.

Finally, covered with dust, we arrived at the two-room unpainted house on the small ranch worked by Uncle Joe, an uncle I did not remember having seen before. He was a handsome man with eyes so brown they looked black. During supper the adults all laughed about the bullet hole in the house. While cleaning his gun, Uncle Joe had accidentally fired a shot that narrowly missed Aunt Dora, who had been working in the kitchen.

After supper, while my father and his sister reminisced about their childhood, Uncle Joe saddled a horse—Aunt Dora's transportation to her school—so I could ride around a freshly mown field. The horse ignored me, trotting around with my seat slapping on the saddle. Now and then, on some whim over which I had no control, it jumped haycocks. This was scary, but I didn't mind. I was riding a real horse on a real, though very small, ranch. Wait till school started and I could brag to Ralph!

That night the three of us slept out under the stars, and during the night, coyotes howled. Very early the next morning, as the sun was rising over the mountains to the east of Prineville, we drove on along a narrow empty road. "I wonder," remarked Mother, "if that bullet that came so close to Dora really was an accident."

Dad was silent for a while before he said, "I don't like her living out there on that place so far from anyone." For some reason I did not understand, none of the family liked Uncle Joe, but everyone loved Aunt Dora. Uncle Joe was an intense, unsmiling man, different from my uncles related by blood, but he was kind to me. The family's dislike puzzled me.

Suddenly Dad shouted and stepped on the

brake. A mule deer had leaped out of the juniper trees and now stood in the middle of the road, staring at us. We stared back for one astonished moment before it bounded on into the junipers on the opposite side of the road.

"Well, I'll be—!" said Dad.

"Wasn't it beautiful?" said Mother.

We were all silent, wonderstruck by that one frozen moment. Then we drove on toward Portland.

The Platoon System

When school started in September, girls discovered that boys, awful in the sixth grade, had become terrible in the seventh grade. They said bad words, some of which we did not understand. They tucked small mirrors under the laces of their Keds and stuck their feet under girls' skirts.

Our class was supposed to be studying grammar, which included diagraming sentences from a tan book, *Grammar and Composition,* by Effie B. McFadden, with selections for seventh-grade study and memorizing. Many of us referred to this unpopular book simply as "Effie."

"After all, this is a grammar school," Miss Stone, our serious teacher, reminded us when we groaned at Effie and her grammar.

Instead of concentrating on Effie, my attention

turned to a curly-haired boy named Allen who sat across the aisle from me and was more interesting than making skeletons out of sentences and labeling the bones with proper subjects, verbs, objects, and modifiers.

Allen was also more interesting than our arithmetic book, obviously the work of an educator who enjoyed torturing seventh-graders with "An ice cream can was $2/3$ full. After 18 dishes had been taken out, it was still $1/16$ full. How many dishes had been taken out?" Concealing Allen's notes from Miss Stone, who threatened to read aloud any note she intercepted, was my exercise in problem solving.

Because boys usually went in pairs for protection when one of them was interested in a girl, Allen and his friend George sometimes walked home from school with me while I wheeled my bicycle. Except for chinning themselves on any handy branch, they were almost civilized. It was George who gave me his first manual training project, a breadboard nicely rounded at one end, with a neatly bored hole for hanging it on a nail. Mother put it away for me to use "someday," and whenever she ran across it, she referred to it as "Beverly's hope chest."

In the seventh grade, changes took place, not only in boys but in the school curriculum. The platoon system was introduced. This meant we were taught some subjects—"Effie," reading, arithmetic, and United States history—in our homeroom but marched off in platoons to other rooms for music, art, nature study, library, an oddly named class called "auditorium," and double periods for domestic science or manual training. And, of course, gymnasium, where seventh-graders exercised with wands or marched while Claudine played "Napoleon's Last Charge" on the piano.

Girls sewed in 7A and cooked in 7B while boys hammered, sawed, and sanded in another basement classroom. Many parents objected to the platoon system; schools should stick to basics. Mother felt the new system too strenuous. "It's just rush, rush, rush all day long," she said. At PTA she complained to Miss Stone that my handwriting had deteriorated and was difficult to read. Miss Stone replied that before long most people would use typewriters.

We now had a school library with a librarian, Miss Smith, a young, brisk, well-tailored teacher who also taught reading. She taught us how to use the library and once made us line up alphabetically by our last names, as if we were books on shelves. After that, I found a place on the shelf where my book would be if I ever wrote a book, which I doubted.

Miss Smith introduced an innovation to Fernwood. Until Miss Smith entered our lives, our teachers forbade reading in the classroom, except for old copies of the *National Geographic*. No one enjoyed this except the terrible boys who knew, by ragged covers, which issues contained pictures of naked women in African tribes.

Not being able to read in school had frustrated me. During the first week, I held my reader under my desk and read it all the way through, even though teachers said repeatedly, "Do not read ahead." After that I hid books I wanted to read inside my geography, an ideal book, because of its size, for hiding other books. I was deeply grateful to Miss Smith, not only for letting us read but for letting me into the library first on the days when *St. Nicholas* magazine arrived.

Miss Smith had standards. We could read, but we must read good books. Cheap series books, traded around the neighborhood, were not permitted in her classroom. Miss Smith was also strict. She once made me stay after school until I could write on the blackboard, from memory and in order, all the presidents of the United States. I do not recall what I did to deserve this judgment, but I do recall thinking it more sensible than writing "I will not talk in gymnasium" one hundred times—a penalty once meted out by Miss Helliwell, our gym teacher.

Miss Smith also gave unusual assignments.

Once, without warning, she said, "I want you to pretend you live in George Washington's time and write a letter to someone describing an experience."

Write something we had not learned in a book? This was unheard of. "But that's not fair," some protested.

Miss Smith assured us that such an assignment was perfectly fair. We knew she was right. Miss Smith was always fair. Strict, but fair.

"You mean *now?*" someone asked.

"Now." Miss Smith was always firm.

"But how?" someone else asked.

"Use your imaginations," said Miss Smith, unconcerned by the consternation she had created.

I was excited. All my life, Mother had told me to use my imagination, but I had never expected to be asked, or even allowed, to use it in school. After a moment of pencil chewing, I wrote to an imaginary cousin, telling how I had sacrificed my pet chicken to help feed Washington's starving, freezing troops at Valley Forge.

The next day, Miss Smith read my letter to the class, praised me for using my imagination, and said everyone else in the class had to try again. At Fernwood any written work, even practice sentences, that did not measure up to teachers' standards was rewritten—sometimes more than once. Smugly I read a library book while my

176

classmates struggled with letters about their sacrifices of pet lambs and calves for Washington's troops. Copycats, I thought with contempt. Mother had told me authors found their ideas in their own minds, not in the words of others. Besides, who ever heard of lambs and calves in the middle of winter? In Yamhill, they were born in springtime.

Next Miss Smith gave us homework: writing an essay about our favorite book character. This brought forth groans and sighs of resignation from most of the class. Nobody wanted to do homework, especially original homework.

That weekend, Mother happened to be visiting her parents in Banks, where Grandpa Atlee had bought back his store. (When he was seventy, after two years of retirement, he decided he was too young to be idle.) After I put together a Sunday dinner for my father, who gamely ate it and was enjoying his pipe and the Sunday paper, I sat down to write the essay. Which favorite character when I had so many? Peter Pan? Judy from *Daddy-Long-Legs?* Tom Sawyer? I finally solved this problem by writing about a girl who went to Bookland and talked to several of my favorite characters. I wrote on and on, inventing conversations that the characters might have had with a strange girl. As rain beat against the windows, a feeling of peace came over me as I wrote far beyond the required length of the essay. I had discovered the pleasure of writing, and to this day, whenever it rains, I feel the urge to write. Most of my books are written in winter.

As much as I enjoyed writing it, I thought "Journey Through Bookland" was a poor story because the girl's journey turned out to be a dream; and if there was anything I disliked, it was a good story that ended up as a dream. Authors of such stories, including Lewis Carroll, were cheating, I felt, because they could not think of any other conclusion.

I was also worried because I had used characters from published books. Miss Smith had lectured us on plagiarism and said that stealing from books was every bit as wrong as stealing from a store. But how could I write about a favorite character without having him speak?

When we turned our essays in during library, I watched anxiously as Miss Smith riffled through the papers. Was I going to catch it? Miss Smith pulled out a paper that I recognized as mine and began to read aloud. My mouth was dry and my stomach felt twisted. When she finished, she paused. My heart pounded. Then Miss Smith said, "When Beverly grows up, she should write children's books."

I was dumbfounded. Miss Smith was praising my story-essay with words that pointed to my future, a misty time I rarely even thought about. I was not used to praise. Mother did not compliment me. Now I was not only being praised in front of the whole class but was receiving approval that was to give direction to my life. The class seemed impressed.

When I reported all this to Mother, she said, "If you are going to become a writer, you must have a steady way of earning your living." This sound advice was followed by a thoughtful pause before she continued, "I have always wanted to write myself."

My career decision was lightly made. The Rose City Branch Library—quiet, tastefully furnished, filled with books and flowers—immediately came to mind. I wanted to work in such a place, so I would become a librarian.

Miss Smith, dear brisk lady who gave unusual assignments, astonished us again by announcing one day that we were no longer to call her Miss Smith. She was now Mrs. Weaver.

"You mean you got *married?*" we asked after this news had sunk in.

With a smile, she admitted she had. A teacher getting married was unheard of to us. Some were called "Mrs.," but we thought they were widows. Our teachers never discussed their personal lives with their classes, but here was a teacher who had presumably fallen in love while she was a teacher. Astounding! Such a thing had never happened before and, in the course of my education, never happened again.

In addition to Mrs. Weaver and her surprising assignments, home economics and manual training were new to us. In sewing class, while boys were sawing away at their breadboards, girls in 7A were laboring over samplers of stitches and seams and putting them to use making cooking aprons that slipped over our heads and had bias binding properly applied to the neck and armholes, and bloomers that taught us to measure elastic without stretching it. In 7B, cooking class began by making white sauce without lumps.

Mother, who often told me how she sacrificed to give me piano lessons, gave up when we moved from Hancock Street; so once again I had school music to dread. *That* had not changed. We were still expected to sing alone.

The goals of our new art class were conformity and following directions, not creativity. The teacher passed out squared paper. She instructed us to set our pencil points on an intersection ten squares down and four squares from the left-hand edge. Her directions droned on. "Draw a line two squares over, one square down, two squares over . . ." on and on. Grimly we labored to keep up with the instructions, to pay her the attention she demanded. When she finished, those of us who had kept up had identical outlines of a rooster. We were then told which crayons to use "without scrubbing" on which squares; others, those who did not pay attention or, in the case of the terrible boys, did not want to, had something surreal. Perhaps, without knowing it, they had captured the spirit of a rooster, if not the approval of the art teacher.

Auditorium was taught by Miss Viola Harrington, who stood at the rear of the auditorium while we took turns standing up straight, walking up the steps to the center of the stage, facing her, and whispering, "Can you hear me whisper?"

"Louder," said Miss Harrington. "I can't hear you."

We took deep breaths and even deeper breaths until we thought our lungs would burst, until Miss Harrington could hear us at the back of the auditorium.

From that stage, speaking distinctly, we recited memorized poetry, reported on current events, and gave talks on assigned subjects. When Miss Harrington assigned me a report on "Guano," Mother said, "The idea! What a thing to talk about in public." The terrible boys whispered a different word for fertilizer supplied by birds on islands off the coast of South America. I was embarrassed to stand on the stage talking about bird droppings, no matter how rich in nitrate and phosphate. Such stuff, to me, was not valuable but something to avoid stepping in. Miss Harrington obviously had never walked across a barnyard full of chickens.

The most unusual change in curriculum was nature study, taught by Miss Lydia Crawford, an aloof eccentric with long, glossy brown hair wound around her head and with the high color and glowing complexion of an outdoor woman. She always wore plain dark dresses that stopped just below her knees; she wore high brown shoes, much higher than those I had finally been allowed to abandon, which laced all the way to her knees. We were all intimidated by Miss Crawford.

Miss Crawford believed that if we were to study nature, we should have nature around us. She brought, and encouraged us to bring, exhibits to be placed on a ledge beneath the window. Plants bloomed; lichen, mosses, and minerals were displayed; chipmunks raced on wheels; and a two-headed garter snake and I stared at each other through the glass walls of its prison.

Miss Crawford told us that when she was a little girl, she was taught to recite "From the stable to the table, dirty flies!" She said women ruined their skins with face powder, which was made from talc. "See, children, this is what foolish women rub on their faces," she said, holding up a piece of the greenish mineral while her own face shone from soap and water. She told us we must always rotate our crops and never, never perjure ourselves.

The curriculum required Miss Crawford to lead us through a book with a dark blue cover entitled *Healthy Living*. We stared listlessly at drawings of correct and incorrect posture and of properly balanced meals before we began a relentless journey of a meal through the alimentary canal, beginning with food thoroughly chewed. I endured what went on in our mouths and esophagi, but I began to have doubts about the whole thing down around our stomachs, and when we reached the liver and gallbladder, the whole messy business became disgusting and, beyond those organs, too embarrassing to mention. I did not want to think of all that going on inside of *me*. Ugh.

Miss Crawford, radiating health, was apparently as bored with *Healthy Living* as her class. One day she suddenly closed the sensible text, laid it aside, and with her fingertips resting on the front desk in the center row, began to tell us a story about a man named Jean Valjean, who lived in France a long time ago and who had spent nineteen years as a galley slave for stealing a loaf of bread to feed his hungry nieces and nephews. We all perked up. We knew about galley slaves from pirate movies.

Miss Crawford's cheeks grew redder, and her face became incandescent with excitement, as she went on and on, telling us the story in great detail. Nothing this moving had ever happened in school before. We groaned when the bell rang.

"Children," said Miss Crawford, "I shall continue the story in our next class."

Nature study became the best part of school. Chipmunks still raced, a home of a trapdoor spider was added to the nature display; but all that mattered to us was *Les Misérables.* On and on we traveled with Jean Valjean, hounded by Inspector Javert all the way. Fantine, her little daughter, Cosette, and the wicked Thénardiers all became as real as, perhaps more real than, our neighbors. We gasped when Fantine sold her beautiful hair to pay the Thénardiers for the care of Cosette. Even the most terrible boys sat still, fascinated. Unaware of social injustice in our own country, we were gripped by Victor Hugo's story of social injustice in nineteenth-century France.

Some parents—but not mine—listening to us retell at the supper table the marvelous story Miss Crawford was bringing to our imaginations, began to object. Storytelling in school was improper. We were there to learn, not to be entertained. Telephone calls and visits were made to Mr. Dorman, who was a very wise man. Of course we should be studying *Healthy Living,* and so we did. However, at least once a week Miss Crawford came to our auditorium class to continue the story.

June came, summer vacation was about to begin, and she had not finished *Les Misérables.*

"Don't worry, children," she said. "I'll be here when you return in September."

True to her word, Miss Crawford was waiting when school started, and took up where she had left off. Well into the eighth grade, the story of Jean Valjean came to an end. Miss Crawford began another novel by Victor Hugo, *Toilers of the Sea.*

By coincidence, the next year one of Mother's cousins, Verna, who had become a librarian, sent me a copy of *Les Misérables,* which she inscribed in her beautiful vertical handwriting: "A book that you may enjoy someday, if not now, Beverly." I had already lived the book and did not read it for many years. Then, as I read, Miss Crawford was before me on every page. She seemed not to have missed a single word.

I often wonder why this particular book meant so much to an eccentric Oregon teacher. Had someone in her family suffered a terrible injustice? Had her repeated warning about perjury come from some experience in her own life? Or had she perhaps spent her childhood in isolation on a farm where the works of Victor Hugo were the only books available? And why did she suddenly feel compelled to share this novel with a class of seventh-graders? Whatever her reasons, I am profoundly grateful to her—and to the wisdom of Mr. Dorman for circumventing unimaginative parents and allowing her to tell the entire book in such detail. My copy has 1,222 pages.

Uncle Joe

Aunt Dora and Uncle Joe, because of her health, moved from sagebrush country to a farm near Molalla, about thirty miles from Portland. Aunt Dora invited us out to see a rodeo, the annual Molalla Roundup. I found this invitation exciting, something to brag about to Ralph.

When we arrived in Molalla on a hot summer day, Uncle Joe said he had been unable to buy five seats together. He offered to sit with me so my parents and Aunt Dora could sit together and visit. Uncle Joe and I climbed to the top of the bleachers while the others sat down in front.

The heat was unusual for Oregon. Cowboys riding bucking broncos and roping steers churned up clouds of dust. The spectacle was sweaty, dirty, and, at first, fascinating. Gradually it grew monotonous and the heat and dust stifling.

Uncle Joe bought me a bottle of Orange Crush, which I held in one hand as I drank through a straw. Uncle Joe took my other hand in his. Having my hand held did not seem unusual. In Yamhill, I had often walked down the street with an uncle holding me by the hand. However, because of the heat, I wiggled my hand free of his. I could not make conversation with this uncle and was glad when the rodeo ended.

On the ride home, Mother remarked, "It does seem odd that Joe could not get five seats together."

Dad said, "I thought so, too."

I did not bother to mention Uncle Joe's trying to hold my hand. The incident was dropped. It seemed of no importance.

That winter, Aunt Dora invited us to come out to Molalla for Saturday dinner, a midday meal on the farm. We could spend the night and drive home on Sunday. Mother, tired of cooking, accepted with pleasure. Dad looked forward to exploring the farm. I took a book with me.

Saturday night, after I went upstairs to bed in the cold farmhouse and lay shivering, weighed down by heavy woolen quilts while my body warmed the sheets, Uncle Joe burst into the room, thrust a folded sheet of paper into my hand, planted an urgent tobacco-smelling kiss on my cheek, and said, "For God's sake, don't show this to anyone!" and left. I was terrified.

Innocent of any knowledge of sex, I knew something very wrong was occurring. I was too frightened to get out of bed, fumble in the dark for the overhead light, and read what was written on the paper. Uncle Joe might burst in again if he saw a light. My stomach churned in fear, and I scrubbed my cheek with the sheet. This was not uncle behavior. All my other uncles were kindly, affectionate men, but they did not sneak into my bedroom to shove notes at me or kiss me in the dark.

When my parents came upstairs, I heard Mother say, "Why don't we take Dora and Joe back to town with us?"

"No!" I called out in a whisper. "Please, please, don't!"

Neither parent caught my fear. "It will make a nice change for Dora," said Mother, who was always sympathetic to farm women.

"She works pretty hard out here," agreed my father as they went into another bedroom and closed the door. I lay in fear of the man who had become an evil stranger.

In the morning, Uncle Joe did not take his eyes off me, but I managed to whisper to Mother,

"Please don't take them back with us. *Please* don't."

Mother merely gave me an impatient look. I could not find an opportunity, or was too frightened, to read the letter. Uncle Joe was watching every move I made.

That day I rode back to Portland in anguished silence between Mother and Aunt Dora, the letter clutched in my hand inside my pocket, while Aunt Dora and Uncle Joe made plans to take Mother and me to a movie the next day before they caught the bus back to Molalla. I spoke up. "I don't want to go to a movie."

Dad was beginning to be irritated by my behavior. "Of course you want to go to a movie," he said.

Still I could not bring myself to read that letter. I am not sure why. I know it repelled me. Perhaps I was afraid of what I might find in it. That night I slept on a cot in the attic because my room was used as a guest room. Monday morning I stayed upstairs as long as I dared, listening to the sounds from below.

When Mother and Aunt Dora were in my bedroom, and Uncle Joe was in the living room, I ventured downstairs and into the kitchen, where I finally got up my courage to unfold the letter, a sheet of tablet paper filled with pencil writing. I caught the last words, "Your lover, Joe," before

190

the writer of the letter was beside me, his dark eyes glittering like coal.

I fled to the bedroom and sat down on the bed with the letter crushed in my fist behind my back, while Mother and Aunt Dora continued their conversation, oblivious to my distress. Uncle Joe followed and sat down on the bed beside me. Smiling at the women, he twisted my arm and pried the letter from my fingers. I shrank from him.

"Why, what's the matter?" Mother asked at last.

Uncle Joe answered for me. "I just wanted to know what Beverly wanted for Christmas." A lie. This branch of the family did not exchange Christmas gifts.

Aunt Dora kindly asked what I wanted for Christmas. I couldn't think of anything. Uncle Joe announced he felt like going for a walk. The women continued their discussion of clothes. I did not want to speak out in front of my aunt.

When time came to leave for the movie, Uncle Joe returned.

For once I defied Mother. "I will not go to the movie."

"Of course you will," she informed me, her mouth tightening into a straight line.

"No I won't," I contradicted.

To avoid a scene, Mother had to give in. The

three of them left, and I was alone, trying to sort out my frightened thoughts.

However, true to habit, halfway to the corner, Mother made some excuse for returning to the house. She was furious. "Beverly, I don't know what gets into you sometimes!" she began. "It wouldn't hurt you to be nice to your aunt and uncle. You don't often see them, and they think a lot of you. How can you be so selfish?"

"I am not selfish," I said, angry because no one had listened to me and upset at being accused of not being nice to my aunt, whom I loved.

I told her about the kiss, the letter, my twisted arm, the way she and Dad ignored my agitation.

Now Mother had to listen. She was appalled at what she heard. "Beverly, I am sorry. I had no idea" was all she could say as she hurried off to prevent her in-laws from returning to see what had happened to her.

That evening, Mother was heartsick and said she could hardly bear to sit through the movie beside Joe. "Poor Dora," she said. "Married to that man."

Dad was furious when he heard the story. "I always knew Joe was no good," he stormed. Sometime after he had calmed down, he must have told my aunt what had happened, for after my experience, none of my girl cousins was ever

192

left alone in a room with Uncle Joe, and he was watched whenever he was near.

I never saw my lovely aunt again, but when I was married, she sent me an antique quilt made with tiny, tiny stitches; and once after Joe's death, when she was very old, she wrote me a letter in exquisite penmanship answering some questions about family history Mother had passed on to her.

The most puzzling part of this unpleasant episode of my girlhood was Mother's failure to give me any information about sex. My understanding of the word "lover" came from fairy tales read when I was younger, and yet I sensed from Uncle Joe's behavior, from his glittering dark eyes, that the word had a meaning I did not understand and that the meaning held evil for me.

Badly frightened, without understanding exactly what I was frightened of, I did not know how to ask.

Eighth Grade

Our class was changing. A quiet boy who sat in front of me had so much trouble with arithmetic that he began to cry during an important test. The tears of a boy thirteen years old distressed me so much that, for the second and last time, I cheated in school. I slipped him some answers.

A bitter, scowling boy across the aisle from me spent his days drawing, in elaborate detail, guns and battleships. He made me uneasy, and perhaps made Mrs. Drake, our eighth-grade teacher, uneasy, too, for she left him alone. Teachers were there to teach, not to solve, or even discuss, personal problems.

The boys who were so awful in the sixth grade and terrible in the seventh grade became really *horrible* in the eighth grade. They belched; they farted; they dropped garter snakes through the basement windows into the girls' lavatory. In the days before zippers, a boy could, with one swipe of his hand, unbutton the fly of another boy's corduroy knickers—always in front of girls who, of course, nearly *died* of embarrassment while the red-faced victim turned his back to button up. Mrs. Drake said, "Something has been going on, and you know what I am talking about, that has to stop." When Mrs. Drake was not looking, "something" went right on.

The horrible boys, whose favorite epithet was "horse collars!" shouted "Hubba-hubba!" at any girl whose developing breasts were beginning to push out her blouse.

Some girls changed, too, and were considered "fast" because they took to wearing lipstick and passing around two books, *The Sheik* and *Honey Lou: The Love Wrecker,* books I scorned. These they ostentatiously read on "those certain days" when they sat on a bench in the gymnasium while the rest of us twirled the Indian clubs or marched while Claudine pounded away at "Napoleon's Last Charge" on the battered piano.

I was engrossed in *Jane Eyre,* but Claudine peeked into *The Sheik* and reported, "Gee, kid, there was this sheik who kidnapped this girl and carried her off to his tent in the desert. He laid her on a bed, and when she woke up in the morning, he was gone, and then she discovered a dent on the pillow next to her, and she knew he had slept in the same bed with her. Wow!' Our innocent imaginations were incapable of filling in the crux of this scene. A dent in the pillow was shocking enough. Yipes!

The horrible boys refused to accept the lessons in conformity the art teacher was struggling to teach. This time we were taught to letter, first on squared paper and then in cut-out letters. We cut out, all in blue-green and pale orange paper, the silhouette of the entrance to the Oregon Caves and the words "Oregon Caves," which we pasted to the front of manila folders to hold our essays for open house. However, some of the boys rebelled by rubbing their rulers hard and fast against the edge of the table in the art room. They did not set the tables on fire, but they did produce smoke, which impressed me. As a Camp Fire Girl, I had been unable to start a fire by rubbing two sticks together. Our teacher refused to give in and send the boys to the principal's office.

Boys were worst of all on the days girls had cooking lessons. We brought most of our ingredients from home in our cooking baskets, neatly covered with clean napkins. Whatever we cooked we took home—if we could get it there. As soon as school was out, hordes of ravening boys, who had spent their double period of manual training working up appetites while sniffing cooking odors, descended on the girls. I tried to make a quick getaway, pedaling furiously on my bicycle with wooden wheel rims warped by sun and rain, while horrible boys grabbed at the basket swinging from the handlebars. Sometimes I succeeded.

Girls were beginning to rebel, too, making Miss Campbell, our thin, harrassed domestic science teacher, the victim. Miss Campbell's favorite word was "tend," as in "White sauce tends to lump if not adequately stirred." When she announced that our class was to give a demonstration on table setting and napkin folding at a PTA meeting, she learned that many girls tended to object.

"That's not fair," someone said. "You can't make us stay after school when we haven't done anything wrong."

"Boys don't have to stay after school," someone else said. "Boys can get away with anything they want."

A girl named Joanne, a blonde who lisped, defied Miss Campbell. She stood up and said, "You can't make me thtay after thcool," and walked out of the basement classroom. Miss Campbell ran after her, leaving the rest of us humming with excitement. What would happen to Joanne? Would she be expelled?

Miss Campbell, looking grim, returned alone. The next domestic science period, Joanne was in class, but she did not stay after school to take part in the demonstration.

Teacher-pleaser that I was, who also felt sorry for Miss Campbell, I did not object to folding a napkin for the PTA and was assigned the hardest part of all, the proper way to fold a large damask dinner napkin, which I pretended to iron at an ironing board set up on the stage.

"Always iron the right side of the napkin last," I said, educating our mothers and teachers. "This tends to polish the design in the damask."

I held up the folded napkin to polite applause from the audience and, I suspect, to the relief of Miss Campbell, who, during the remainder of the year, was faced with teaching us the correct way to patch a garment, work a neat buttonhole, darn a sock so it wasn't lumpy, and make a dress.

Mother, a pillar of the PTA, was dissatisfied with school. Not enough homework was assigned, a complaint she had made since I was in the third grade. If we didn't rush about from room to room, we would learn more. Perhaps she felt that folding a damask napkin in domestic science was not sufficiently intellectual. When she was a girl, this was taught at home, not in school. She announced she was going to visit school to see for herself what was going on.

I was horrified. School visits by mothers were for the first and second grades, not the eighth grade. I could not live down such a visit, ever. I would *die*.

"You won't do anything of the kind," said Mother. "Mr. Dorman says parents are welcome anytime."

Why didn't nice Mr. Dorman keep his mouth shut at PTA? I lived in dread of Mother's being as good as her word and bringing disgrace down upon me. But the visit never took place.

Mother and Dad had worries more serious than what went on at Fernwood. Each evening after I left the dinner table to read the newspaper, they lingered over tea and spoke in worried voices of subjects that did not interest me—high tariffs, the stock market, Wall Street, banking.

Dad began to come home from work with his shoulders stooped, his face heavy with worry.

Some Portland banks closed their doors when too many depositors began to withdraw money. What if this happened to the bank where he worked? That year the West Coast National Bank did not give its annual Christmas bonus, a frightening omen. We depended on that bonus and had plans for every cent.

As it turned out, the bank was bought by the larger United States National Bank, an institution that promised to keep the West Coast employees. Dad had me sell the two shares of West Coast stock he had once given me, and with the proceeds bought me, at a great bargain, an ancient typewriter with an extra-long carriage for typing bank forms. I would need it when I became a writer.

Dad moved next door to his former bank to stand on another marble floor. We feared a run of worried depositors withdrawing all their money from this bank, where my father was responsible for order in the lobby.

And then in October 1929 the stock market crashed. Except for school, everything seemed to come to a halt. All around us, men began to lose their jobs. The Miles family lost their money in the stock market. Grandpa Atlee wrote that the logging camps and lumber mills around Banks were shutting down, an ominous sign, for Oregon's economy depended on the lumber industry.

At school we charted estimated expenses for a family of four with an income of $2,500 to $3,000 a year. We learned to write checks, borrow money, read interest tables, and compound interest semiannually. We learned the difference between stocks and bonds; we studied real estate as an investment, property insurance, and income tax.

The Stone Arithmetic Advanced told us, concerning income tax: "In 1924 the *normal rate* on incomes up to $6000 is 2% less the amount of the exemption." Mother looked at my arithmetic book and remarked with bitterness, "There aren't many people around here who earn six thousand dollars a year these days."

In spite of what was going on in the country, Fernwood trained us to save money. One of the banks started a school banking program with a teller, the boy who was best in arithmetic, in each class. We brought our bank books to school, along with nickels, dimes, and quarters to deposit in our accounts. One boy often brought a whole dollar. Speculation on the size of his account was the talk of the class.

Mrs. Drake gave us lessons in algebra to ease us into high school mathematics. "Your teachers won't spoon-feed you the way I do," she warned us.

In reading, we studied a chapter of *The Mill on the Floss,* by George Eliot; another from *Moby-Dick,* by Herman Melville; Robert Browning's "Incident of the French Camp"; Abraham Lincoln's "Address at the Dedication of the Gettysburg National Cemetery"; and Alfred, Lord Tennyson's "Flower in the Crannied Wall." Mrs. Weaver required the memorizing of "If," by Rudyard Kipling. We hated it. The only twentieth-century selections I can recall were short stories by O. Henry—"The Gift of the Magi" and "The

Ransom of Red Chief"—but of course the century was only twenty-nine years old at that time.

That winter I became ill once more, with what was assumed to be influenza—in those days almost any sickness was called the flu or grippe. When fever, weakness, and sore throat persisted, Mother finally called a doctor. He examined me, felt my glands, leaned on the foot of the bed, and asked, "Mother, does she know about the moon?"

Weak as I was, I was infuriated. He spoke as if I were absent or deaf, he addressed my mother as if she were his mother, and he insulted my intelligence by his silly reference to "the moon."

I knew very well he was referring to monthly periods. Why didn't the stupid man say what he meant? And what business was it of his, anyway? The old snoop. Mother was angry because he charged five dollars for the visit, even though he had to pass our house on his way to his office, and because he did nothing to help me recover.

After I had been in bed two weeks, Mother sent me back to school because, she later ruefully admitted, she was worn out taking care of me. I felt so weak I paused to rest against every fire hydrant along the way and almost immediately had to return home for another two weeks of fever and weakness, lying in my great-grandfather's four-poster bed, looking out at rain and sleet. Mother began to read me *The Little Minister,* by

James M. Barrie, because for once I felt unequal to reading. Halfway through, she laid it aside. I finished it a few pages at a time.

After my illness—whatever it was, it would be my last for many years—I looked so bedraggled that Mother bought me rouge for my pale cheeks and, every morning before school, insisted on curling the ends of my hair with a curling iron heated over the flame of a burner on the gas stove.

"Yow, you're burning my neck!"

"Stand still a minute, can't you?"

The odor of singed hair filled the kitchen when Mother overheated the curling iron. By the time I had walked to school, because bicycle riding was unsophisticated for an eighth-grade girl, the damp air had usually wilted my curls.

The lingering debilitation of illness subdued me to the point of studying harder, with the result that, on one report card day, Mrs. Drake announced that I was the only member of the class to earn straight E's for Excellent. No one at school held this against me, but Mother said, "You see? You could always earn straight E's if you would only apply yourself."

About that time, Mrs. Drake confided that she was taking a course in short-story writing. Because she was taking this course, we should write, too, a paragraph of description. The class groaned.

After some thought, I recalled the moment when the mule deer sprang out of the juniper trees and hesitated in front of our car as the sun was rising over the mountains. I handed in a short paragraph entitled "Sunrise on the High Desert."

My description was returned to me inflamed with red pencil corrections. Mrs. Drake had changed almost every word. This was a shock. After so much encouragement from Mrs. Weaver, I did not know what to think.

Mother, in a day when parents supported teachers, merely remarked that she did not agree with some of Mrs. Drake's corrections, but she kept the paragraph. Years later, after I had published several books, I ran across it. The morning sun in the clear, cold desert air I had described as "blazing"—not a particularly good word—as it rose above the juniper trees. Mrs. Drake crossed out "blazing" and wrote in "burning," apparently believing that "burning" was the only acceptable modifier for a desert sun, even the sun on a cold Oregon morning. Perhaps she had read *The Sheik*.

In a negative way, this experience influenced my writing. For years I avoided writing description, and children told me they liked my books "because there isn't any description in them."

Toward spring, Mother began to tell the neighbors, "Beverly has finally begun to perk up," and a good thing, too, for Miss Helliwell had us hang up our Indian clubs and begin to rehearse calisthenics, identical to those taught in gymnasiums all over Portland, until the important day when girls dressed in white middies and black gym bloomers and boys in white gym suits marched to the Grant High School Bowl. There we joined hundreds of pupils from all over the city and performed, under the leadership of the tan, muscular superintendent of physical education, the calisthenics in which we had been drilled. In a yellowing newspaper photograph, we look more like the youth of Germany than of Oregon.

About this time I wore Mother down and was allowed to shed forever my woolen underwear, and in the nick of time, because I had to try on the dress I was making in domestic science so Miss Campbell could mark the hem. Now my underwear would not show.

Our eighth-grade graduation took place in our classroom without parents present. From my seat by the window I could see Mount Hood, which was out on that sunny June day. (In Portland we spoke of Mount Hood as being "out" on clear days, as if it had popped out of the ground like a gopher.) The class waited, excited and expectant, for Mr. Dorman, who finally arrived, carrying a handful of paper diplomas, to make a short, friendly speech. Fernwood had prepared us to be good citizens, he told us.

With forty and sometimes more pupils in a class, our teachers had taught us the fundamentals of survival in society. Every one of us could read. We had learned to speak distinctly and correctly and to cope with the arithmetic necessary for daily life. Girls were capable of making their own clothing—not that many wanted to—and to prepare simple, nutritious meals. Boys had learned basic carpentry, and some had even built tables with hand-rubbed finishes, which we all admired as they proudly bore them home on the last day of manual training.

School was a businesslike place. Teachers and parents expected us to learn but not to think for ourselves; we expected to be taught. Our textbooks were practical-looking and of a size comfortable for the hands of children in the grades in which they were used. No one, not even ourselves, expected school to amuse us, to be fun, or to be responsible for personal problems. The appreciation of music and art would have been considered expensive and unnecessary by parents.

Of the sixteen teachers who taught us in eight

years, most were pleasant, firm, and impersonal, which was the attitude we expected of teachers. The Gregory Heights director of the PTA program was never my teacher, only a painful childhood memory. She and Miss Falb, who switched my hands with her bamboo pointer, were the only teachers who ever touched me, but I probably leaned against Miss Marius because I loved her so much.

As I listened to Mr. Dorman and walked to the front of the room to accept my diploma, I was already imagining myself in the long corridors of the Ulysses S. Grant High School.

With our diplomas, Mr. Dorman handed each of us a small buff card, our first adult library card, a symbol marking the end of childhood.

At the age of six I dislike this yellow organdy dress because it is scratchy. Mother is ashamed of my socks. We move to Portland shortly after this picture is taken.

ABOVE: *Two Halsey Street sisters stand to my left on the day I enter the first grade. I am anxious because one girl is prepared with flowers for the teacher and I am not. Will the teacher like me?*

RIGHT: *At age seven my Yamhill smile begins to fade. Mother is disappointed because my socks show in this picture, paid for with a free coupon.*

ABOVE: Grandpa and Grandma Atlee stand apart in their general merchandise store. I peek into the right of the picture. Mother, who destroyed almost all pictures of herself, removed herself from this one with scissors.

LEFT: In the fourth grade Evelyn, the older girl who played "Rustle of Spring," and I are outfitted as tin soldiers for the operetta. Our puttees slip and have to be rewound, but we make it through the performance.

ABOVE: Mother's determination holds our lives together in this house on Thirty-seventh Street.

RIGHT: When I am in the eighth grade, a friend's mother suggests taking this picture of me for a Christmas present to Mother, who, instead of being pleased, is angry. She has told me to avoid this friend, whom she considers "common."

A Summer of Change

The summer of 1930 began happily. Claudine and I, after my family moved to Thirty-seventh Street, became friends. I learned that she was a talented pianist and plump from lack of exercise because her kneecaps sometimes slipped out of place, causing her to fall.

The first thing we decided to do, on a warm summer day when the air of Portland was rich with the rotten-cabbage smell of paper mills, was use our new adult library cards.

We timidly approached the adult half of the book collection, choosing almost at random before we slipped back to the children's side of the room for old favorites.

After the library, Claudine and I went to the drugstore for Cokes before we walked back to her house, where we settled ourselves on her taupe mohair davenport to read in companionable silence.

But then, in a week or so, Claudine and her mother went out to the Pudding River, which they referred to as Puddin', where the Klums had a cabin. The Miles girls all seemed busy and did not invite me to their house. I was lonely but not discontented. The library supplied me with books. High school lay ahead.

One evening, when Mother and Dad were drinking their tea and I was reading the newspaper in the living room, I sensed a terrible icy silence settle over our house, a silence that chilled me with fear. Something was wrong, terribly wrong.

Mother broke the silence with one syllable of despair. "Oh!" I heard Dad push back his chair, go into the bedroom, quietly shut the door, and throw himself on the bed. Why? I was terrified.

Mother came into the living room. "Daddy has lost his job," she said softly. "The bank is dismissing the employees it took over from the West Coast National and has given them two weeks' notice."

The Depression had come to us. Mother cleared the table and washed the dishes alone. I sensed she preferred solitude to help. I sat filled with anguish, unable to read, unable to do anything.

When Dad finally emerged from the bedroom, I felt so awkward I did not know what to say or even how to look at him. To pretend nothing had happened seemed wrong, but seeing him so defeated and ashamed of defeat, even though he was not to blame, was so painful that I could not speak. How could anyone do such a thing to my father, who was so good, kind, reliable, and honest?

That summer of 1930 was terrible for all three of us. My father wrote letters of application, applied for jobs in person, called on businessmen who had been friendly to him in the bank lobby, and asked if they had an opening or knew of one. Nothing. A man whose life had been farming had little to offer in the city but willingness to work, loyalty, a dignified appearance, and a gracious manner. "Mr. Bunn is a real gentleman" was often said of my father. In Portland his intelligence had been wasted.

Every workday morning he left the house. Late in the afternoon he came home with his shoulders sagging, his footsteps heavy.

Mother searched his face. "Well?" she always questioned.

"Nothing" was his answer. Everywhere men were being laid off, not hired.

The money in our bank account and the last paycheck must be stretched as far as they would stretch, for every penny counted. Mother fidgeted, figuring on the backs of envelopes: so much to be set aside for property taxes, so much for my carfare to the orthodontist, and when she calculated that bus and streetcar fare cost less than the expenses of driving the car, so much for carfare for my father to look for work.

Mother took inventory of the cupboards, planned Spartan meals—macaroni and cheese, Spanish rice, creamed chipped beef on toast. Because our kitchen had bins for sugar and flour, we had bought these staples in hundred-pound sacks. Fortunately, the bins were full. Mother began to bake our own bread and, for her insatiable sweet tooth, cake, following recipes calling for one egg and the least amount of shortening. She ran out of vanilla and started to use a bottle of almond flavoring a large bottle. We ate almond-flavored cake; almond-flavored cornstarch, tapioca, and bread puddings; almond-flavored cookies and custard. Mother even made almond-flavored fudge, until she used up all the chocolate. Then, as long as the brown sugar lasted, she made almond-flavored penuche. The Depression, for me, took on the flavor of almond, and to this day I dislike any almond-flavored dessert. When we ran out of tea, my parents drank hot water with supper. We brushed our teeth with baking soda to save the cost of toothpaste. Someone told my

219

father how to sharpen the blade of a safety razor on the inside of a straight-sided drinking glass. Making one blade last became a challenge. We stopped spending the weekly nickel on *The Saturday Evening Post,* to the disappointment of the boy who earned a few cents delivering it.

Evenings, my father carried a wicker chair out to the front porch, where he sat alone in the long Oregon dusk, sheltered from view by a curtain of Virginia creeper that hung from a wire between the porch pillars, whistling softly to himself, filling every tune with sorrow. Mother and I ached for my father in his despair, and I still grieve when I hear "Bedelia" or "Smile Awhile," and, most heart-wrenching of all, a song about "the West, a nest, and you, dear."

I felt so claustrophobic at home that I made my trips to the orthodontist last as long as I dared, wandering through Meier & Frank's department store looking at all the merchandise I could not buy. Almost every day I walked to the library, choosing books for Mother as well as for myself and lingering until I knew Mother would begin to worry.

Early August brought a welcome invitation. The Browns, who had once lived in the Halsey Street neighborhood, invited me to go to their mountain cabin for the weekend as company for their daughter Elizabeth. Elizabeth and I slept on cots in a tent pitched in huckleberry brush under ancient fir and hemlock trees.

That weekend was idle and restful. My tension drained away. As Elizabeth and I lay on our stomachs on a flat rock beside a stream that flowed through maidenhair fern past the cabin and on into the Zigzag River, we watched rainbow trout laze in the pool below. Like boys in Norman Rockwell covers on *The Saturday Evening Post,* we tried fishing with string and bent pins, but the trout were indifferent.

Sunday came. As time approached for Mr. Brown to drive me into Portland, leaving Mrs. Brown and Elizabeth behind, I began to dread going home. I wanted—was desperate—to stay in the mountains, and so I did the unforgivable, according to Mother's standards. I asked if I could stay longer. Mrs. Brown kindly said I could stay for a week.

Elizabeth had a saddle horse, Brownie, which kept her busy. While she was riding or grooming her horse, I lay in a hammock, staring up at bits of sky visible through the sieve of evergreen branches, swaying gently, thinking of nothing at all. Sometimes I wandered through the woods, chanting as I had learned to chant in our eighth-grade study of poetry:

Thís ĭs thĕ fór-ĕst prĭ-mé-văl. Thĕ múr-mŭr-ĭng pínes ănd thĕ hém-lŏcks . . .

One day, Mrs. Brown rented a horse for me, so I could go riding with a high school girl whose mother packed us a lunch that included two cantaloupes. We mounted our horses, which I called our "trusty steeds," and rode off across the Zigzag River into a logged-off area where second-growth timber was beginning to rise out of the magenta blossoms of fireweed. We talked sporadically about life in Grant High School: which were the best courses, who were the favorite teachers, all that I could look forward to.

Still clutching our cantaloupes, we rode on until we came to a ghost logging camp, where we dismounted to eat an early lunch. Carrying cantaloupes on horseback was not practical, we decided. We ate near a decaying shanty that still bore a crude sign: "Haircuts two bits. Bring your own hair and shears."

Then we rode on aimlessly, up a steep corduroy logging road made of slab wood wide enough for wagon wheels and now silver with age and weather. The sun warmed and relaxed my back.

In midafternoon we turned back, the horses' hooves slipping on the silver road. We did not know where we were; we trusted our horses to take us safely back to the cabins, which they did. I felt I wanted to ride on forever.

At the end of the week, on the highway back to Portland with Mr. Brown, I prayed my father had found work. He had not. Worse, my parents were angry with each other, which filled me with a fear and sadness I had never before experienced. There had been tension over the sale of the farm, but at that time each understood and sympathized with the other.

This was something different. They argued in front of me. Dad said we would have to sell the house. Mother said flatly, "No we won't. We'll pull through somehow. We have to. If we let go of this house, we are lost."

Finally Mother gave in. "Go ahead and advertise it," she said in a voice stiff with anger, "if you must."

Dad placed an advertisement in the Sunday paper, calling the house a bungalow. "Bungalow!" said Mother to me when he was out of hearing. "This is no bungalow. Bungalows are those cheap little houses out in Parkrose." She loved her house and was fiercely proud of every inch, from the plate-glass windows in the living room and dining room to the hardwood floors. "The oak came from Siberia," she always explained when they were admired.

That Sunday was a long, terrible day while we waited for the telephone to ring. It remained silent, so silent that its failure to ring became a jangle to our nerves. At the end of the day, I sensed Mother's triumph. No one was buying houses; some were losing theirs because they could not meet mortgage payments. We would hang on to ours as long as we could.

My father gave up smoking his pipe to save a few cents. Then he sold the car. I felt, as he must have felt, that we were trapped in Portland forever.

With the sale of the car, I balked at the long walk to Sunday School, where Dad had driven me and picked me up afterward.

"But you must go to Sunday School," said Mother.

"Why?" I asked. "You and Daddy haven't gone to church since Yamhill."

"I don't have the clothes for church" was Mother's excuse.

"Do you go to church to worship God?" I asked. "Or do you go to worship clothes?"

Mother laughed and relented. "You have a point," she said, "and it is a long walk in bad weather." Spending money on bus fare was out of the question, and then there was the collection plate to think of.

As August wore on with no sign of work, my father grew more depressed and irritable. Late one afternoon, when Mother asked him if he would like potato soup for supper, he flew into a rage. "Don't ask me questions like that!" he shouted. "Don't expect me to make such deci-

sions! If you do, I'll eat my meals in restaurants!"
He went into the bedroom, slammed the door,
and began to sob.

Mother and I sat motionless, helpless, and sick.
Then Mother said in a weary voice, "He would
have to make decisions in restaurants." We both
knew there was no money for restaurants.

Finally Mother quietly made the soup, but neither of us had any appetite. I thought of the revolver that still hung on my parents' bedpost, and
of the bullets that lay on the dresser, and was
filled with fear.

Late that evening my father finally came out,
looking drawn and exhausted. Mother said softly,
"Lloyd, sit down and smoke your pipe." He
smoked in silence and seemed to take comfort.

It's not his fault, I thought in anger. *It's not
his fault.*

I excused myself and went to bed, where I tried
to soothe myself by thinking of the mountains,
the calm of the woods, the graceful trout. Re-
membering helped, but I felt as if all three of us
had forgotten how to smile. I vowed that I would
never ask my parents for anything that cost
money, a vow I kept.

Mother wondered how she could earn money,
but in those hard times no one would hire a married woman. Jobs went to men for the support of
families. She did, however, work on the election

225

board and help take the 1930 United States census. After entering many contests, she won two dollars for Honorable Mention in naming a new brand of bread.

High School Freshmen

"Well, well, so you girls are going to be frosh," a neighbor said to Claudine and me when school was about to start. We exchanged knowing, amused looks. What an old-fashioned word, "frosh"! We were freshmen.

Having grown both up and out, I was now medium-sized, but my clothes were not. Everything I owned, except the sunburst pleated skirt, which Mother had insisted I buy to grow into, was either too short or too tight.

A neighbor gave Mother an old pink woolen dress, which she successfully made over into a jumper for me. She contrived a cream-colored blouse from something found in a trunk in the attic. One of her friends, now married to an eastern Oregon wheat rancher, had a daughter older than I who passed on two nice dresses. In our neighborhood, no girl would dream of entering high school in half socks. I used hoarded nickels and dimes to buy silk stockings. Five dollars from my Arizona uncle bought a raincoat.

Claudine was more fortunate. Mrs. Klum solved her wardrobe problem by buying her three knit dresses, at five dollars apiece. Three new dresses, not hand-me-downs, and all at one time; the Miles girls, passing their clothes to one another, and I were awed by such luxury. We began admiring one another's clothes by saying, "Is it new, or new to you?"

Then the Depression came to Claudine's house, for Mr. Klum, a steam fitter, lost his job when construction came to a halt. A family friend offered him a job as a night watchman at a pharmaceutical company at a small salary he was not too proud to accept. My father had no close friends, only acquaintances.

And so, the day after Labor Day, when smoke from forest fires dimmed the atmosphere, the sun was a sullen orange ball, and ash drifted over the city, Claudine and I walked on our silken legs up the steps of Ulysses S. Grant High School, where we both were enrolled in a college preparatory course—with no possibility of college. "Things will get better in four years," Mother

228

said with her usual determination. "They have to."

As we entered the building, Claudine and I tried to pretend our insecurity was invisible. Everyone else looked so confident, mature, and sophisticated. Girls wore lipstick. Some even pinned up their long hair. Boys in long, dirty, cream-colored corduroy pants with ink lines doodled between the ridges of the fabric seemed worldly because they had resisted their mothers and washing machines.

The horrible boys from the eighth grade suddenly looked subdued and self-conscious in their new, clean corduroy pants. Some, poor things, still wore knickers and probably suffered as much as girls who wore lisle instead of silk stockings.

Grant High School, Claudine and I soon discovered, was not the friendly, tolerant place that Fernwood had been. Grant was snobbish and full of cliques. Sororities and fraternities with silly initiation rites dominated the social life. Girls were admired for being cute, peppy, and well-to-do, and, most of all, for driving cars. Popularity required energy I lacked. All I wanted was a few good friends. Claudine was occupied with her music.

Grant High School arranged everything possible in alphabetical order. Claudine and I went in different directions to find our registration rooms, which we quickly learned to refer to as our "reg rooms." I was filed with students whose last names began with *A* or *B,* while Claudine took her place with *J* and *K.* Since the boy alphabetized in front of me and I were enrolled in many of the same classes, I went through four years of high school staring at the back of his neck, which I came to know very well. It was a slender, sensitive neck that supported an intelligent head of softly curling brown hair. I grew fond of that neck and of the boy it belonged to.

Life was better at school than at home. Grant High had excellent teachers—well-informed, efficient, strict, and caring—although I had some doubts about a couple of coaches who taught history and seemed to have a prejudice against girls. Except for English, I worked just hard enough to keep Mother from nagging; but on the whole, I enjoyed school, but not physical education, taught by a woman who wore blue rompers and long cotton stockings. I never succeeded in learning to climb a rope, and thought volleyball was tiresome. When trapped into playing basketball, I made my own rule: always run away from the ball. No one ever complained, or, as far as I know, noticed.

In freshman English, tiny Miss Hart led us through *Treasure Island,* which pleased the boys.

The book bored me. This was followed by *As You Like It* and *Silas Marner*. We also waded into a compact little green book, *The Century Handbook of Writing*, by Garland Greever and Easley Jones, a valuable book that was to accompany us for four years. Completeness of thought, unity of thought, emphasis, grammar, diction, spelling, "manuscript, etc.," and punctuation—we went over it all every year.

Claudine and I, who were inclined to giggle at almost anything, found *The Century Handbook* entertaining. We often quoted examples. If I said, "Phone me this evening," she replied, " 'Phone. A contraction not employed in formal writing. Say *telephone.*' "

After a test, one of us quoted, " 'If I pass (and I may),' said Hazel, 'let's celebrate.' " This, from a rule on the use of quotation marks, was worth a fit of giggles.

Mother insisted on coaching me in Latin, the foundation of the English language, she kept telling me. I liked the sound of Latin and danced around chanting, *"Amo, amas, amat,"* but Mother could not understand my listless attitude toward declensions and ablative absolutes. Mother loved Latin, truly loved it, and coaching me took her mind off her troubles. She also kept an eye on my algebra and wanted to study along with me. I flatly refused her company. If there is one thing a fourteen-year-old girl does not want, it is her mother studying algebra with her.

We also studied poetry and discovered Carl Sandburg, so different from Kipling and his moralizing "If" and the nineteenth-century poets we had studied in grammar school. No rhymes, and it was still poetry. What a relief! We were required to write a poem, and after reading "Chicago," the class was inspired to rousers such as

> Portland.
> Shipper of wheat,
> Grower of roses.
>
> Oregon.
> Feller of trees,
> Catcher of salmon.

We also memorized one hundred lines of poetry of our own choice, a requirement for each year of high school.

For an assignment in original writing, I wrote a little story, "The Diary of a Tree-Sitter," following Mother's advice, "Make it funny," and "Always remember, the best writing is simple writing." Sitting in trees, on houses, or atop poles to set records was popular at the time. My story was based on an incident in the *Journal* and had the advantage of not having to be concerned with spelling. When the paper was returned, Miss Hart had written, "E+. This is very funny. I hope it is original. You show talent." I was ecstatic.

The inspiration for my next story, "The Green Christmas," was a newspaper account of a boy who fell into a river below a dye works that dumped green dye into the water. In my story, being dyed green saved the boy from playing the part of an angel in a Christmas program at church. To my surprise, Miss Burns, the chairman of the English Department, called me out of class to ask where I got the idea for the story. Puzzled, I explained the source of each part. She told me she had wanted to make sure the story was original. I was a little hurt that she could think it might not be original.

"The Green Christmas" was published in the *Grantonian,* the school paper, but another girl's name was given as the author. I did not hesitate to point out, in indignation, the error. A correction appeared in the next issue, but somehow that small boxed paragraph was not the same as seeing my name on my own story, a story which, much altered, became a chapter in my first book.

The recognition I was winning at school helped balance the unhappiness at home. My father still had not found work. Money from the sale of the car was running low. The house was always cold, as wood and coal were fed sparingly into the furnace to try to make it last through the winter.

Then one day, Meier & Frank's green delivery truck pulled up in front of our house. The driver handed my surprised mother a package with her name on it. "What on earth . . ." she puzzled as she tore off the wrapping. The package contained a ham sent by my father's sister Minnie. Mother smiled, it seemed to me, for the first time in days. "Minnie always knows just what to do," she said, and Aunt Minnie always did know. She was that kind of aunt.

We ate ham baked, fried, ground, made into a loaf with plenty of bread crumbs, scalloped with potatoes; and when we were finally down to split-pea soup made with the bone, Dad came home smiling. In the darkest Depression, he had actually found work managing the safe-deposit vault at the Bank of California. The vault, with its heavy steel door and time lock, was located in the basement. It was a sad place for a man who had spent so much of his life working outdoors in the Willamette Valley. But the job brought home a paycheck, smaller than he had earned before, but one that put food on the table, made mortgage payments, and paid taxes. We were luckier than many. Dad whistled to a livelier beat and ordered a few more sacks of coal.

The Pukwudjies

When we moved from Hancock to Thirty-seventh Street, I transferred to a Camp Fire group, the Pukwudjies, an Indian word for "little people," in our new neighborhood. We were a group of eight, including Claudine and three of the five Miles girls, led by Lucy Grow, the childless wife of a physician whose lungs had been damaged by gas during the war. Mrs. Grow was short, rotund, with sparse dyed hair, cut short, that stood straight up. She was the first married woman I had ever known who did not devote her life to being a good house-wife. For this she was considered eccentric. Mrs. Grow thought much that went on in Camp Fire Girls was nonsense and said so, but she recognized the importance of such an organization for girls "too old for toys and too young for boys."

The Pukwudjies took turns meeting at one another's houses, where our mothers provided refreshments. We never looked forward to one girl's house because her mother, who believed in plain living, handed each of us a simple, nutritious apple. My mother served warm gingerbread with whipped cream or cream puffs with hot chocolate. "Girls always enjoy whipped cream," she said, and she was right.

Mrs. Grow was full of ideas. She gave us a course in first aid and taught us how to bind a book. She drove a big old Franklin sedan that could hold the whole group, and sometimes, in good weather, she drove us out to Canyon Road to cook our supper over a bonfire in a clearing. We charred kabobs, baked bread-on-a-stick (biscuit dough wound around a stick that always, because of our impatience, turned out slightly raw in the middle), and ate vegetables wrapped in cabbage leaves for salad. We enjoyed the meal, which we topped off by toasting or charring marshmallows. Mrs. Grow was a woman of courage who did not fuss about details.

When Mrs. Grow told us the administration of Camp Fire Girls was offering a five-dollar prize for the best linoleum-block print cover for their bulletin, she suggested we try. I attacked a square of battleship linoleum with my father's jackknife and produced a cover of sorts. Once again I won a prize, not because my cover had any artistic merit, but because no one else entered the contest. I saved my five dollars for a bathing suit.

Mrs. Grow was concerned about the Pukwudjies she was shepherding through the Depression. When Camp Fire headquarters announced a contest with a prize of a free week at Camp Namanu the next summer for the group that earned the most points, Mrs. Grow said, "There is no reason why you girls shouldn't win." She organized us.

Points were given for visiting factories. Mrs. Grow packed us into her Franklin, and we took off to surprise owners of small factories by our sudden interest in their products. In one afternoon we whipped through a pencil factory, a spaghetti factory, a candy shop where chocolates were dipped (free samples!), and, of course, the Jantzen Knitting Mills, that haven for any adult stuck with providing an educational experience for a group of the young in Portland. I was fascinated by a woman who stretched knit fabric over a lighted glass panel and circled flaws with chalk and by the razor-sharp, whizzing machine that cut out stacks of bathing suits at one time.

Another method of earning points was writing a letter to a Camp Fire Girl in another city. Mrs. Grow gathered us around Claudine's dining room table (brownies for refreshments), where we combined our efforts to compose a joint letter, which Claudine's aunt, who worked in an office, mimeographed for us. The next week, on someone else's dining room table, we shared and signed a ream of letters which Mrs. Grow shipped off to Camp Fire headquarters in other cities, to be passed around to other groups. We earned a lot of points that way and did not break any rules. We also received credit for answers. I heard from a girl in Minnesota and from another in England.

Camp Fire headquarters was upset when our group turned in the most points. Another group was expected to win. We were accused of violating, if not the rules, the spirit of Camp Fire. "Nonsense!" said Mrs. Grow, who had once handed a traffic officer a nickel and told him to go buy himself an ice cream cone, and was not easily intimidated. The discussion grew more heated, with Mrs. Grow defending her girls, who needed that week at camp. There was no rule against mimeographed letters, no rule against visiting more than one factory in one day.

Mrs. Grow was so feisty that headquarters had to relent and award us the prize. The other group was also given a free week because they were true, in winning their points, to the spirit of Camp Fire—something as vague as the requirements for the Namanu Honor I had failed to earn on my first trip to camp. We Pukwudjies did not mind sharing the glory of the prize, even though we caused hard feelings at headquarters. We would have our week, free of the Depression, and camp with friends would be fun. Those of us who could not find hand-me-down blue middies went to work making our own out of the cheapest blue cotton we could find.

The Pukwudjies, in our homemade middies and black gym bloomers, enjoyed our week at Camp Namanu, where Mrs. Grow came to visit and once more found a loophole in a rule. Eating between meals was strictly forbidden in our cabins, so she invited us all to the counselors' lodge, where she gave us each a candy bar. We were shocked at this violation of rules. "Eating between meals is not forbidden counselors," she said. "Why should it be forbidden you girls?" We ate with wicked pleasure, not at all in the spirit of Camp Fire.

Campers at Namanu had a custom, whenever a girl was late for a meal, of singing at the top of our voices, "You're always behind like an old cow's tail." One member of our group, a girl who was always neat, punctual, and efficient, discovered one day she was going to be late for dinner. Rather than face what she felt was the humiliation of being sung to, she skipped the meal—one of Namanu's greater crimes—and hid. No counselor missed her. At the final evening camp fire, when she was awarded Namanu's highest honor, the Namanu Girl Honor, some of our group were bitter about this injustice, but I was already hardened, from my early experience, to Namanu's honor system.

What mattered to me was the carefree feeling I enjoyed that week. This time, Mother had not sacrificed to send me to camp. I had come to dread Mother's sacrifices for me because they made me feel so guilty.

Depression Summer

The Depression grew worse. More men lost their jobs. Almost every day, at least one defeated man came to the door trying to sell shoelaces or pencils to earn a few cents. At first Mother bought from them because we were lucky. My father had a job. But finally so many came to the door she could no longer face the sad, gray men. We hid when we saw them coming. Mother always grieved when we did this. "You see what heroes men are," she said.

All around us, people were having a hard time. A neighbor took in her nephew, a child about five years old. Anger spilled out of her house, and sometimes, after dark, she would lock the little boy outside as a punishment. He ran from the back door to the front door and back again,

241

pounding with his fists and sobbing, "Let me in! Let me in!"

When I went to bed, I hid my head under the pillow to shut out the sound of the child's sobs until his aunt relented and unlocked the door for him.

Summer was lonely. Claudine went to Puddin'. The Miles girls, those near my age, went out to the homestead their parents had claimed from land returned to the government by the railroad. There they raised and canned food and cut wood for life in the city.

I combined trips to the orthodontist with knitting lessons at Meier & Frank and trips to the main library to stretch twenty cents' carfare as far as possible and keep me away from home for an afternoon.

Halfway through the summer, Uncle Guy, Mother's older brother, and Aunt Ida arrived by automobile all the way from Arizona, bringing presents—a turquoise and silver Indian bracelet for me and chunks of turquoise from my uncle's mine for Mother. Uncle Guy, tanned and fit, seemed untouched by the Depression, and during his visit, Mother became her old vivacious self. When my aunt and uncle drove out to Banks to visit my grandparents and Uncle Henry for a few days, I went along. Grandpa Atlee had built a post office for Banks so Uncle Henry could have a job as postmaster.

My grandfather's store, which never seemed to change, was a two-story wooden building with "W. S. Atlee General Merchandise" painted across its false front. Living quarters and Grandma Atlee's little millinery shop were above the store. My grandparents' day began with someone pounding on the front door, demanding, "Open up!"

"All right, all right, I'm coming. Hold your horses!" Grandpa shouted as he pulled up his suspenders and hurried down the stairs.

From the time the door was unlocked, old men gathered in the store to discuss politics and spit tobacco juice ("eatin' tobaccy," they called it) into the stove while they waited for the train to arrive and for Uncle Henry to sort the mail so they could read their newspapers. Their sentences often began with "I see by the paper . . ." or "Will Rogers says . . ." That summer there was talk of loggers out of work, lumber mills that had shut down, and the possibility of a chain store opening in Forest Grove. Grandpa worried about competition from one of the new chain stores. Men asked Uncle Guy, "How are things going down there in Arizona?"

Drummers, as traveling salesmen were called, arrived. My grandmother, wearing a black sateen apron over her blue housedress, hurried down-stairs to order dry goods—notions, stockings, underwear, and yard goods—for her side of the store, while Grandpa placed his orders for coffee, tea, rice, crackers, chewing tobacco, and all the items carried on his side. He bought orange wheels of Tillamook cheese and, from farmers, eggs, which he let me candle to test for freshness by holding each over a hole in a wooden box that contained an electric light. If the egg appeared translucent, it was fresh. At the back of the store, coal oil for kerosene lamps was kept in a drum with a spigot, from which customers' coal oil cans were filled, and a half a potato was jammed on the spout to prevent spillage.

Customers came in for spools of thread, overalls (pronounced "overhauls"), coffee, which Grandpa ground in a red coffee mill, tea, and crackers sold in bulk from red metal bins. The cash register rang, but some customers, shamefaced, asked that their meager purchases be "put on the books." My grandfather obligingly charged the items, often knowing he would never be paid. He said, "I can't see little young 'uns go without." He had only contempt for people who bought tinned vegetables when they could grow their own. At noon my grandparents took turns going upstairs for a hasty lunch—usually canned Vienna sausage, bread and cheese, and coffee, which Grandpa "saucered and blowed" in his private deep saucer. He did not have time to let his coffee cool in a cup.

Afternoons, women came in for their small purchases. If they were buying percale for housedresses, Grandma, with kindly patience, laid their patterns out on the inexpensive fabric, arranging and rearranging the tissue-paper pieces to save every inch of material for women who were so pinched for money. They could no longer afford to retrim their hats each season, so Grandma's boxes of ostrich plumes, now out of fashion, grew dusty along with the ribbons, bolts of veiling, artificial flowers, and cherries that had delighted me when I was younger.

Evenings, people in Banks dropped into the store to chat and enjoy a bit of company, to discuss politics and harvest, and to exchange gossip. Women, except during berry harvest, led lonely lives. When the berries were ripe, the town came alive.

Strawberries were picked by Filipinos and taken to a warehouse with an open side where women hulled berries and packed them in barrels between layers of sugar for shipment by train to New York. All of Banks was perfumed by crushed ripe strawberries, and that summer, in the evenings after a field had been stripped of berries, I went with my two uncles into the fields and ate dark, ripe berries, rich with juice, that had been overlooked. Uncle Guy said there was nothing like the fields of Oregon berries in Arizona.

When the last customer drifted away and my grandfather locked the store, we climbed the stairs to the living quarters, where Grandpa snapped on his radio to listen to the Alka-Seltzer news at ten o'clock. He turned his radio on a few minutes before ten in case the news came on early, and when the program began with the fizz of an Alka-Seltzer tablet dropped into water, he always said, "Yep, there she goes!" After the news, bed, and in the morning, another pounding on the door.

My grandparents' whole lives were lived in that old tinder-dry building with its one staircase leading past the drum of kerosene. Grandma cooked on a wood range and often gave the fire a fast start with a splash of coal oil from a can beside the stove. Somehow the store, the center of community life in Banks, never caught fire.

When Uncle Guy and Aunt Ida took me back to Portland and were saying goodbye, Uncle Guy ran his hand over my head and said, "She'd be a good-looking chick if she had a permanent wave."

Mother smiled and said, "She's a little young. She has plenty of time for that." I was inclined to agree. A permanent wave was something else that somehow belonged in the mysterious future. When Uncle Guy left, Mother wept.

My uncle's remark made me look at myself in the mirror and fiddle with my hair. What was the use? I would never look nice with my mouth full of metal and wire. Mother began to look thoughtfully at me. The week before school started, she said, "Why don't you spend the five dollars your uncle gave you on a permanent wave?"

Well! A bit of the future had appeared through the mist.

Mother sent me to a neighborhood hairdresser, an experience fraught with suspense. The woman, widowed or divorced, who had sons to support, could afford neither a license nor a proper shop. She operated her business illegally in her dining room and lived in fear of a city inspector finding out about it. If someone rang the doorbell, customers were instructed to run and hide in the bathroom while she hid evidence of her business.

The woman shampooed my hair while I bent forward over the bathroom washbasin. Then, in the dining room, she pulled strands through slits in felt pads and wound them so tightly around metal rods I felt as if my eyebrows were raised. Next she soaked my hair with evil-smelling liquid and fastened to each roller clamps that dangled from a heavy electric machine. The electricity was turned on. What if the inspector rang the doorbell? How could I run and hide when I was fastened to this hot, heavy contraption? Would the hairdresser leave me? Would my hair burn off? Would she be fined, even arrested? Then how would she earn her living? A permanent wave gave me plenty to worry about.

The machine heated and turned into an instrument of torture. I was silent as long as I could bear the heat. Then a small "Ooh!" escaped.

"Where does it burn?" the hairdresser asked. I pointed. She aimed a blower at the spot. My whole head seemed to be burning. I pointed; she blew. "It won't be long now," she said over and over. The ordeal seemed to take forever. Somehow I got through it all without the inspector calling and without my hair being burned off. When the clamps were removed and my hair unwound in a Medusa-like tangle, it was neutralized, shampooed again, set, and dried. I looked in the mirror. This rite of passage, this trial by permanent wave, left me feeling better about myself, and the hairdresser still had her illegal business, which helped her survive the Depression.

Mothers and Daughters

When I think of my mother now, I remember her as I so often saw her when I came home from high school. She is lying on the davenport, her legs covered with a blanket, a magazine fallen to the floor beside her. This is another day when Mother feels blue. She worries constantly, unable to recover from the days when Dad was out of work. She seems unable to get warm.

A fly buzzes against the window. Mother throws back the blanket and springs to her feet. "Get that pesky fly!" she cries and seizes the nearest weapon, a newspaper that she rolls up. The chase is on. Thump. Whack. "Beverly, help me get that pesky fly before it spots the windows!" The fly grows angrier, Mother more determined, while I continue to stand, schoolbooks clasped to my chest, fascinated by the drama of Mother versus the fly.

Thwack. "There," she says, triumphant. "I got him!" The corpse is brushed from the sill and tossed to an ashy grave in the fireplace.

"That's the end of him," she says in satisfaction. Her adrenaline is flowing once more. She folds the blanket, picks up the magazine, and sits down on the davenport. "Now tell me about your day at school," she says. I tell her, making an ordinary school day as amusing as I can. I feel responsible for Mother's happiness because she sacrifices for me.

Mother and I, relieved of maintaining peace to protect my father during the terrible days when he was out of work, were now free to disagree with each other.

Nothing I did pleased Mother; nothing she did pleased me. I wanted to wear lipstick. She said, "Certainly not. Lipstick on young girls is vulgar."

"But I wear rouge."

"That's different, and you don't wear much, just enough so you won't look peaked."

School had taught me always to fold paper, as well as damask napkins, neatly; she left the newspaper in a crumpled heap on the floor. I wanted to do my homework in the evening; she wanted me to do it immediately after school "to get it out of the way." I never touched the piano, and after she had sacrificed to give me lessons; I reminded her she no longer touched it herself.

Mother's requests began, "I am going to have you ..." I did not mind cleaning up my room, dusting, making the salad, but I resented her manner of asking me.

When spring came, I wanted to wear bobby socks like the other girls. On a trip to the orthodontist, I detoured from my usual route to buy, with twenty-five cents saved a nickel at a time, a pair of red bobby socks at Woolworth's. Mother made me return them on my next trip overtown.

Risking Mother's disapproval of lipstick on young girls, I bought a tube of Tangee lipstick at the dime store and applied it the minute I got home from the orthodontist.

At supper, my parents apparently did not notice the lipstick. No comment was made. Finally I announced, in case they had not noticed, "I am wearing lipstick."

"So we see," said Mother, her lips tightening into the straight line I was beginning to dread more than anything in the world. I gave up lipstick. It was not worth Mother's devastating disapproval, no matter how much I needed to make little decisions of my own.

Mother made me a white dress and a red jacket. The two halves of the collar were tied in a bow, the ends of which hung down over the jacket at the back of my neck. I thought the collar fetching, but Mother said the bow looked too heavy and wanted to cut it off. I protested. One day, when I came home from school, I discovered that Mother had amputated the bow. For once I could not contain my anger. "You had no right to do that," I stormed. "It is my dress, even if you did make it."

Adults of Mother's generation did not believe children should ever cross their parents. Parents were always right. "That dress looked terrible with that bow," she said, not giving an inch. Again her mouth tightened into the thin, disapproving line.

"You have a mouth like a buttonhole!" I hurled at her.

Mother looked stunned. I had often rebelled against her, but this was my first attack. "I'll put the kibosh on you, young lady," she informed me. "You can't talk that way to your betters." We did not speak until supper, when she said to Dad, "Beverly tells me I have a mouth like a buttonhole."

Dad, weary from his day in the basement of the bank, looked at me and said, "Did you say that?"

"Yes, but she—" I did not finish the sentence. My father slapped my face, hard. I left the table and did not speak to my father for two weeks,

252

during which I ate supper in sullen silence and avoided looking at either parent.

As I grew up, both parents had slapped or spanked me, usually for being sassy when I was little or, as I grew older, for talking back. This time I felt I had had enough. I was too old to be slapped by my father. Talking back was not always wrong, I felt, and I would not have spoken such unkind words to Mother if she had left my dress alone and had been willing to listen to me explain my feelings.

I longed to tell my father that I was sorry I had added to the unhappiness in his life, that I understood his irritation and weariness after a day at work; but my generation was never encouraged to talk openly with our parents about feelings. Whenever I tried, I was always judged wrong. This time I did not want to revive a painful episode or involve my father in a silly argument over a bow on the collar of a dress. Neither did I want to be forced to apologize to Mother.

Finally Mother said, "Daddy wants you to know he's sorry he slapped you," and added softly, "You know he loves you more than life itself." I did know.

We went on as if nothing had happened, but after that episode I was careful to avoid confrontations with Mother that would involve my father. His life was hard enough.

I began to spend more and more time at Claudine's house. Mrs. Klum was almost the exact opposite of my mother. She was plump and pretty, with beautiful prematurely white hair. When Claudine and I went into a fit of giggles, she looked up from the Christian Science lesson she was often studying and said affectionately, "Oh, you silly little girls." She did not interfere with Claudine's schoolwork and put no pressure on her to make better grades.

Mrs. Klum and Claudine had mother-daughter arguments, which they usually laughed about in a few days. Although Mr. Klum's income was reduced even more than my father's, Mrs. Klum continued with her bridge club and Eastern Star activities. She and Mr. Klum went dancing at the Masonic Lodge.

Mother objected to my stopping at Claudine's house after school and going there evenings. "If I were you, I wouldn't go to Claudine's house until she comes here," she told me.

"But you and Daddy never go out," I said. "You're always here." Dad spent his evenings smoking his pipe or dozing over the newspaper. Mother read or worked *the Journal* crossword puzzle and yawned.

At supper, Mother announced, "Beverly feels we are not welcome in our own home." She knew very well that what I wanted was a little privacy;

but even more, I wanted, desperately, for my mother and father to have some fun, to have friends, to go to movies—anything. They seemed to have given up happiness.

When Claudine did come to our house, she was made welcome, as were all my friends. Dad sometimes tactfully retired to the breakfast nook with his pipe and newspaper, but Mother dominated. "Do you girls really like jazz?" she asked. "Do you really like Bing Crosby?" We did, of course. Then Mother always said, "Claudine, play something for us." Claudine graciously sat down, rose to twirl the piano stool to the right height, and sat down again to play some popular songs of the day until she and I could escape to the kitchen to make hot chocolate. We could not go to my room as I had planned when we bought the house. My room was too cold, for Mother kept the bedroom doors shut to conserve heat.

At Claudine's house we studied or read together. On a visit to my grandparents, I picked up a book, *Chip, of the Flying U,* by B. M. Bower, a humorous story of a romance between a ranch owner's daughter, a tenderfoot from the East, and a cowhand who turned out to be a distinguished artist of the West. I took the book home and passed it on to Claudine, who read it and said, "That was *good.*" We were both starved for romance.

We enjoyed that book so much we fell in love with the West, which for us was actually East. Oregon did not count as the West.

We discovered that our branch library carried the works of B. M. Bower, an Oregon author, a woman, who wrote Western stories from a woman's point of view. We checked out the books as fast as we could read them: *The Flying U's Last Stand, The Voice at Johnnywater, The Phantom Herd, The Ranch at the Wolverine,* and all the rest.

Saturday evenings, when Claudine's parents were out, we read and hoarded the power of the radio batteries so there would be enough left for us to listen to the songs of the Arizona Wranglers, whom we pictured as a group of cowboys, all looking exactly like Gary Cooper, whose movies we never missed. Gary Cooper was one actor Mother approved of. "His movies are always clean," she said, although later she would not let me see him play opposite Marlene Dietrich in *Morocco.* She had her doubts about Marlene Dietrich.

When we had read all of B. M. Bower, we started in on Zane Grey, a better writer, but one we found funny. A girl disguised as a man was shot. The hero unbuttoned her shirt, and wow! was he surprised! Claudine and I found this hilarious. In one book, the hero fried an egg on a rock, and as he handed it to the heroine, the text read: " 'Eat,' he said." After that, whenever we offered each other something to eat, we quoted in our deepest voices, " 'Eat,' he said," and went off into a gale of giggles.

Mother began to object to our infatuation with the West. I should be reading worthwhile books, Dickens and Thackeray, the books she had read when she was growing up. I pointed out that I had already read *David Copperfield*. She kept an eye on any book I was reading. When I picked up what seemed a rather boring English novel she was reading, she refused to let me finish it because, she said, it was about a woman "who had no modesty." I began to read at Claudine's house the books I was forbidden at home but never understood what it was that Mother did not want me to see.

Although Mother and I had an uncomfortable relationship, her softer moments revealed her hopes for me that told me she might love me even though she showed no tenderness toward me. At these times she looked sad and said to me, "I hope you won't have to scrimp and pinch all your life," or "I hope you will go ahead and be somebody." She also impressed upon me, "Every woman should have some money of her own," and, saddest of all, "I do hope you will marry a man who has the world by the tail."

These touching remarks pointed to a future I was unable to visualize. Everyone had some kind of future, even though in those Depression days many said they did not.

I had no dreams of marriage and few thoughts about boys, although the boys I had grown up with had progressed through the awful, terrible, horrible, and shy stages and had turned into reasonable human beings. They were even courteous, sometimes.

"Wise Fools"

All of Portland felt blue that year. Businesses failed, banks closed their doors to prevent runs, and more weary gray men selling shoelaces or seeking work, any work, rang our doorbell. Mother managed money very, very carefully, but she did buy a bottle of vanilla extract to give us relief from almond flavoring.

Mother and I continued to argue. I needed new school shoes and insisted on brogues like those other girls wore. Nobody wore Buster Brown oxfords or galoshes in high school. Mother stiffened my determination by poking fun at any girl wearing brogues who walked past our house. "Beverly, just come and see how silly that girl looks."

Finally Mother had to admit that thick soles would wear well and keep my feet dry. I got the brogues, wing-tipped, with soles half an inch thick and a fringed tongue that buckled over the laces. I clumped through the next three years of high school in them. Dad polished them for me every Sunday evening.

Claudine and I felt very sophisticated in our brogues as we plodded off to our sophomore year. Nervous freshmen looked immature as they huddled in groups, the chalk dust of grammar schools seeming to cling to them. Boys our age had grown, and their corduroy pants, guarded from their mothers' washing machines, were fashionably dirty. Seniors were less forbidding than they had been a year ago. Our teachers reminded us that the word *sophomore* came from the Greek and meant "wise fool."

Mother was exasperated when I signed up for a course in freehand drawing in addition to English, Latin, mathematics, and biology. I took the course over her objections, but I did not learn to draw, even though the teacher gave me an E, perhaps for properly sharpening a set of pencils for drawing. The teacher was keen on pencil drawing.

Biology showed me with fresh eyes the world of nature around me; and even though we dissected night crawlers with their five pairs of beating hearts, biology was one of my favorite high school subjects. Geometry to me was more interesting than algebra. Mother could not understand my lackluster attitude toward Caesar, his cohorts, and his legions.

The second semester, I decided to take typewriting, which Mother did not consider frivolous because I was going to be a writer. Before the class was allowed to touch typewriters, we memorized the keyboard letters by pounding away on their arrangement printed on heavy paper. When we finally got to real typewriters, which had blank keys, the room was so noisy I understood why the class was hidden away in a corner of the basement. Speed and accuracy were the goals, but for me all the nervous clattering of typewriters and pressure to hit the right keys faster was so exhausting I just managed to squeak through the semester with a grade of G for Good. I could not face the second semester, so I still have to peek to type numbers. Today, when I am asked the most difficult part of writing, I answer "typing," which is taken as a joke. It is not. There is nothing funny about typewriting.

Claudine and I studied *The Century Handbook of Writing*, giggling all the way. Examples seemed even funnier. When we came to Rule 68, "Avoid faulty diction," we studied the examples: *"Nowhere near.* Vulgar for *not nearly." "This here.* Do not use for *this." "Suspicion.* A noun. Never to be used as a verb." Our conversation became sprinkled with gleeful vulgarisms we had never used before. When I announced my presence by noisily tap-dancing on the Klums' wooden porch and probably annoying all the neighbors on the block, Claudine said she was nowhere near ready for school.

"I suspicioned you weren't."

Claudine's reply was something like, "This here shoe-lace broke."

We thought our dialogue hilarious. Mrs. Klum sighed as she looked up from *Science and Health* and said with a smile, "Oh, you silly little girls."

The best part of English that year was the study of the short story, but when the time came to actually write a story, my mind was a blank. The hardest part was having to hand in an outline of a story first. "Make it funny," advised Mother as usual.

I sighed, bit my hangnails, crumpled paper, and when the final day came, turned in an outline of a feeble tale of mistaken identity involving cats instead of people. The outline was returned marked F for Fair, a grade I was unused to receiving. Still, I could not think of anything better. In despair, I wrote the silly story. It was returned with an E–, which I did not think it deserved.

My standards were higher than those of the teacher.

To this day, I cannot outline fiction. I find that

an outline limits the flights of imagination which are the joy of writing. I write and then rewrite, bringing order to the second draft.

In my sophomore year, students with G averages were permitted to join clubs. Claudine, who had escaped Latin because her mother did not care which language she studied, joined the Spanish Club, the Dondelenguas. I chose the Masque and Dagger, a dramatic club that put on a silly play in which I was cast in the role of a debutante. I also joined the Migwan, a literary club whose name we were told was a Dakota Indian word meaning "written thought." I had trouble producing any extracurricular written thought for the meetings, at which we were expected to criticize one another's work. Criticism usually degenerated into an awkward pause until someone ventured, "I think it is very good." I cannot recall a single thing I wrote for Migwan meetings, even though I was a member for three years and served as secretary and president.

Clubs were not our only fun. Claudine and I went by chartered streetcar to high school football games in the Multnomah Stadium, where we yelled for Grant's team as it slithered around in the rain and mud. We walked to the high school gym to cheer the basketball team. We continued to read, study, and listen to the radio, especially "One Man's Family" on Sunday evenings. Claudine, when her parents were out, practiced Gershwin's "Rhapsody in Blue," which she borrowed from the library, instead of "Marche Slav," by Tchaikovsky.

Mother's objections to my spending so much time at Claudine's house grew bitter. "All you girls do is get together and criticize your parents," she complained unfairly. Claudine wasn't critical of her parents. And I was too thoroughly schooled in keeping up a front for the benefit of neighbors to admit any unhappiness at home, even to my closest friend. We had begun to talk about boys—what a boy had said to us by our locker, which was the handsomest, who were the biggest twerps—even though we did not really expect to get to know them outside of school.

One rainy night during Christmas vacation, Claudine and I went with her mother to help deliver Christmas decorations to the Masonic Lodge. Music from a Demolay dance floated down the staircase. While Mrs. Klum arranged her fir boughs downstairs, Claudine and I slipped upstairs into the hall to watch the college-age dancers, like little girls watching a party.

As we sat whispering, a young man in a tuxedo appeared before me, bowed, and asked, "May I have this dance?"

Me? A girl in a woolen school dress and brogues? Claudine poked me. Hypnotized, I rose as the music began and stepped into his arms, terrified. I had never been so close to a boy before. I did not know how to dance. My tongue seemed to fill all the space in my mouth not taken up by bands and wires. As we circled past Claudine, I dared not look at her. I longed for the music to stop, to let me out of this young man's arms, to let me take my icy, sweating hands from his, and let me escape. A boy who smelled so nice did not deserve to have his shoes wrecked.

The music did stop, finally. I gave my partner what was meant to be a smile and left him in the middle of the floor. I grabbed Claudine by the hand and fled the hall. She whispered, "What was it like?"

"Terrible," I said, "but he smelled awfully nice." I was struck by a revelation. "He *shaves.*" Claudine and I went into fits of giggles.

"Oh, you silly little girls," remarked Mrs. Klum.

When I returned home, still laughing, I described my evening to my parents. Mother laughed, too, and Dad chuckled. He rarely laughed, but he had a delightful chuckle.

After that, Mother found the money to enroll me in Mr. Kofeldt's ballroom dancing class at the Irvington Club. She took me overtown to buy me some black pumps with heels and, being a practical woman, made me a red dress sure to be noticed in a crowd. No daughter of hers was going to be a wallflower.

I teetered around the living room in high heels, and on Friday evening I put on my new red dress. Mother and I took the bus to the Irvington Club, where she sat on a bench with another mother or two to watch the class.

The boys, a glum bunch, were neatly dressed in dark suits. They all wore white cotton gloves to prevent their sweaty hands from soiling the girls' dresses. The girls, most of them in dark dresses and praying for tall partners, stood on one side of the room while the boys, praying for short girls, advanced in a horde and made their selections.

Mr. Kofeldt explained the waltz square, which was then demonstrated by his assistants, Mr. Muckler and Miss—(what girl can remember the name of a female dancing assistant, no matter how graceful?). The pianist played "Whispering." Whenever I hear that old tune, I have an almost irresistible urge to rise and go through the waltz square.

If a couple stumbled through the steps or could not keep time to "Whispering," Mr. Kofeldt was beside them, clicking his castanets and telling them not to watch their feet. I learned that the best way to spare the unhappy, dogged boys misery and Mr. Kofeldt's castanets was to lead *them* from my position. For years afterward, dancing partners embarrassed me by asking, "Who's leading, anyway?"

Because 1932 was leap year, Grant High School was giving a leap year dance in the gym. Girls were expected to invite boys, something I had no thought of doing. Although I was being taught, more or less, to dance, the idea of actually going to a dance was so daunting it was not to be considered. School dances were for other people.

Then one day the boy with the sensitive neck turned around to face me. "Why don't you ask me to go to the dance?" he said.

He must be joking. Why else would he say such a thing to me?

He continued to look expectant. I very much wanted to ask him, but I could think of more reasons for not inviting him. How would I get him there? We had no car. I would stumble all over his toes and take over the leading. He wouldn't have a good time, and I would still have to sit behind him while he was thinking of the terrible time he had had at the leap year dance.

I did not know how to answer, so I simply smiled, shook my head, and pretended to be looking for something in my notebook. He turned around, leaving me bemused. Was he teasing?

Was he trying to be funny? Could he possibly have meant what he said?

As Friday nights at the Irvington Club passed, I began to resent the presence of mothers on the sidelines, smiling and whispering behind their hands. Why couldn't I go alone? Because I could not go out alone at night and travel by bus. On the ride home, Mother enjoyed talking over the evening—which boy danced with which girl, who was disappointed, how girls had learned to run past short boys when partners were chosen by the grand-right-and-left, which girl needed a more becoming dress or something done about her hair.

One evening a young man older than the high school boys appeared in the class. He was blond, nice-looking, slender but muscular. Sometime during the evening I found myself plodding through a waltz with him. Neither of us spoke.

Later, when Mother and I were waiting for the bus, the young man offered us a ride home in his Model A Ford coupe with a rumble seat. Mother accepted for us. I felt strange sitting beside a young man and uncomfortable trying to keep my knees away from the gearshift.

Mother was delighted.

First Dates

The next Friday at Mr. Kofeldt's ballroom dancing class, the young man I had met the previous week—whom I shall call Gerhart, for that was not his name—headed straight for me. After the obligatory "May I have this dance?" he clutched me with an arm that felt like iron as he maneuvered me, grimly and silently, through Mr. Kofeldt's steps. Escaping to another partner, no matter how short, was welcome.

When the class was over, Gerhart offered to take Mother and me home again. Mother accepted graciously.

On the way home, Gerhart asked if he could come over Saturday evening to practice dancing. We confessed we did not have a radio, or even a phonograph. For a moment I was terrified that

Mother might offer to play the piano for us. However, Gerhart said he had a radio he could bring. I do not recall which of us, Mother or I, accepted.

The next morning, Mother insisted I had to offer Gerhart something to eat after we practiced dancing. She sent me to the store for a can of chocolate cookies, half a pint of whipping cream, and some maraschino cherries. I whipped the cream, flavored it with vanilla (thank goodness!), spread it on the cookies, stacked them so the cream would soften them, and topped each stack with a cherry.

That evening, Gerhart arrived with his portable radio. The rug was rolled back, my father disappeared into the breakfast nook, and Gerhart led me woodenly through the waltz square and its variations. Mother wandered in and out, playing the part of chaperone and extracting bits of information from him.

Gerhart was twenty-one. He had come from California, where he had completed two years of college. He had a secure civil service job working irregular shifts in a laboratory at exactly the same salary my father earned. Chemistry and physics, two subjects I intended to avoid, were his favorite studies. He lived in a room in a private home, where the daughter of the family had suggested he go to Kofeldt's to learn to dance, and ate his meals in restaurants. Mother overlooked, and I was too naive to recognize, the fact that we had nothing in common.

Mother, feeling I was safe with Gerhart, announced she was going to bed, leaving me to serve a stack of soggy cookies and a cup of hot chocolate waiting in a pan on the stove.

When Gerhart and I sat down at the breakfast nook table, my stomach tightened into a fist. I could think of nothing to say; I could not eat a bite. Because I couldn't eat, he wouldn't. I struggled to think of words to share; Gerhart offered no help. Instead, he laughed at me, which hurt my feelings. Finally, to my relief, he said he guessed he'd better go, and departed, lugging his radio off to his Model A while I returned the soggy cookies to the cooler and, disheartened by the whole experience, went to bed.

Mother, ignoring the touch of cruelty in Gerhart's behavior, found the whole incident hilarious and laughed about it over the telephone with her friends.

I was less amused, but I did brag to Claudine and Lorraine—an older boy, a car, a radio, a good job. They thought I was lucky. Neither of them had ever had a date.

After that, Gerhart pounced each Friday evening at dancing class, brought his radio to our house so we could practice, and finally left it there so we could practice more often. He took me to movies and for a hamburger afterward—a luxury for me, even though I was so nervous I could only nibble at the hamburger.

I continued to go out with Gerhart every weekend and relaxed enough to eat a hamburger. Mother protested. "You are seeing too much of Gerhart. You should go out with other boys."

"What other boys?" I asked. "Nobody else asks me." Somehow I did not care, not because Gerhart meant so much to me, but because I felt I wasn't ready for boys.

"Well, they should," said Mother. "I don't know what's wrong with you." She went on to tell me how popular she had been at my age, as if my lack of popularity were a reflection on her.

I did not refuse Gerhart's invitations. Movies and evenings away from the tensions of home were too tempting. After about three months, Gerhart kissed me at a stoplight.

Being kissed by Gerhart was disappointing. I had expected a kiss to feel more like the time in Yamhill when I stuck my finger in the electric socket, only nice. Still, being kissed was a novelty. I went along with Gerhart's occasional kisses, hoping they would get better. I persuaded myself I was having a good time. Didn't Mother tell her friends what fun I was having? Didn't movies, and stories in *The Ladies' Home Journal,* say girls met boys, kissed, and were happy? Of course I was happy, I insisted to myself, but I did wish Gerhart would not poke fun at activities I enjoyed. He thought English boring, my interest in the literary club silly.

Gerhart also disliked Oregon. He ridiculed the custom of farm housewives drying their washing on porches. I was familiar with old farmhouses without basements, where the porch was the only place to dry clothes in rainy weather. I told him about a time in Yamhill when, waiting days for sun, Mother did a huge washing on the back porch in the electric Maytag washing machine with a wooden tub, her only laborsaving device. She heated water on the kitchen stove and carried it outside, a bucket at a time. When she finished, she hung sheets, towels, and work clothes in the sun on lines in the barnyard. After the last clothespin was in place, the lines broke, and her morning's work fell to the mud. Gerhart thought the story funny. I remembered Mother's tears of despair.

Gerhart also laughed at Oregonians' custom of ordering slab wood by the cord and having it stacked on the strip of grass between the street and the sidewalk. A truck with a gasoline saw cut the wood into furnace lengths, which the man of the house, or boys eager to earn a little money, stacked in the basement beside the coal. Californians could heat their houses with gas, but no one I knew had a gas furnace in Portland. I deeply resented Gerhart's lack of compassion for a life I understood.

Summer came. Mother surprised me by buying me white shoes. I had expected to wear brown oxfords in summer. "White shoes look nice with light dresses," she said, and I agreed.

Claudine went out to Puddin', and Gerhart came to our house whenever work permitted. We passed the time playing two-handed bridge, but he sulked when he lost. I began to let him win to avoid unpleasantness.

Once, when one of us was shuffling cards, Mother asked, "Gerhart, what does your father do?"

Gerhart's face turned hard. He looked straight ahead and said, "He was a house painter who committed suicide."

Mother and I were shocked and sorry. Later she said, "Well, that explains a lot about him." The matter was never mentioned again.

Sometimes Gerhart took me swimming in one of the nearby lakes or rivers. If I returned home with the least touch of sunburn, Mother greeted me angrily with, "You have ruined your complexion." I began to dread coming home from these outings.

One evening, when Mother and I were washing

and wiping the supper dishes, she said, "You know, you are the type that will fade quickly."

What on earth did she mean? This was not a remark of a woman who loved a daughter who had barely begun to bloom. I was too hurt to answer, but after mulling over the remark for several days, I said, "Mother, I don't think it was very nice of you to tell me I would fade quickly. Why did you say a thing like that?"

Mother shrugged. "Well, I said it, didn't I?"

"Well, you shouldn't have!" I snapped.

Mother did not tolerate contradiction. "You should show more respect for your parents," she informed me.

I answered, "Gerhart says one of the reasons he likes me is I am nice to my parents. He says I am not like some girls."

Mother looked surprised and for once had nothing more to say. I was still puzzled and hurt and have often wondered why, when she was so anxious to protect her own youthful appearance, she would direct such a remark to me. Perhaps she envied me my youth. I do not know.

I began to see Gerhart more and more as a way of getting away from Mother. On warm summer evenings we drove to the airport on Swan Island in the Willamette River, which Charles Lindbergh had inspected and pronounced a poor location for an airport. It was a popular spot for waiting to see the ten o'clock mail plane arrive from California. We searched the stars for its lights and, when we found them, followed their descent to the runway and watched the small brave plane that had flown all the way from California taxi to the little terminal. Then Gerhart drove me home.

One day, Mother said, smiling, "You know, Daddy doesn't like Gerhart. I think he's jealous." That my father should be jealous of Gerhart seemed so ridiculous I paid no attention. Mother must be imagining things. However, when Dad bought a radio of our own so Gerhart could take his away, I wondered if he hoped Gerhart would have one less excuse for spending so much time at our house. Perhaps Dad wanted more privacy, I thought.

One day, Gerhart suggested a picnic at the beach. Mother agreed I could go, provided she went along as a chaperone.

"What for?" I asked impatiently. "We don't need to be chaperoned." Hand-holding, a few kisses, mild embraces—that was as far as I ever intended to go. That was the way it was in the movies, and I had no knowledge of what might come later.

Mother ignored me. She set about making a huge bowl of potato salad and suit box full of sandwiches. "People get hungry at the beach," she said.

We set off for a day, with Mother and myself beside Gerhart, and in the rumble seat a wind-tousled, sunburned couple, friends of Gerhart. We often took his friends on outings; my friends were never included.

When Gerhart parked his car among the salal bushes and we carried blankets and the picnic lunch down to the sand and were racing around on the beach, Mother called me back and gave me the only advice or information on sex she ever gave me. "Never play leapfrog with boys," she said. "They might look up."

The Girls' League Show

When my junior year in high school began, I wanted to continue with ballroom dancing because we were about to learn the tango. I pictured myself slinking along like one of Rudolph Valentino's movie partners, a most unrealistic dream because none of the boys in the class would be good slinkers. Gerhart said he had had enough. Mother said I did not need to tango.

I lost the annual lipstick set-to, but I won the debate over my course of study in a year in which we were now given more choice. United States history and English were required, but Mother could not understand why I preferred journalism to solid geometry, though she conceded that it might be of use to a writer. Why I wanted to study French instead of plunging ahead into the pleasures of Cicero and Virgil in Latin was beyond her. "French!" she said. "What on earth is the use of studying French?"

I did not know why I wanted to study French. Perhaps I recalled Mrs. Williams from Halsey Street with her interesting accent and tales of Paris, or perhaps I was thinking of Miss Crawford's telling of *Les Misérables*. No one in our neighborhood expected to actually go to France, and courses were aimed at acquiring a reading, not a speaking, knowledge. I took French.

I also enrolled in a class called "Clothing," an act of self-defense. I had begun to make my own clothes because Mother's sewing was so careless she did not bother to pull out basting threads. School was interesting, more interesting than Gerhart.

Miss Anderson, our journalism teacher, chanted "Who, what, where, when, and why" and "Accuracy, accuracy, accuracy" in a class less structured than any class I had known. Even though I still had trouble with outlines, journalism taught me to set words on paper faster and with better organization than I had been able to do before. Writing "30" at the end of our copy made us all feel very professional.

Junior English, in addition to *The Century Handbook of Writing,* began with mock meetings held in accordance with Roberts' *Rules of Order,* followed by a sentence-by-sentence dissection of Edmund Burke's *Speech on Conciliation with America.*

Debates followed. I do not recall the exact title of my assignment, but it was something like, "Resolved: Chain stores are a menace to society." Inspired by Grandpa Atlee's dread of chain stores, I researched and delivered a stirring speech denouncing chain stores as evil and calling their employees "human automatons." (I smile at this memory whenever a chain store employee notices my name on my check and tells me how much he or she enjoyed my books when growing up.) My partner and I lost the debate, but I was voted best speaker. Grandpa would have called his only granddaughter a humdinger.

And then there was Gerhart, still Gerhart.

I enjoyed high school football games with the rest of the mob, returning home late for supper and hoarse from cheering. I was pleased with my journalism beat—the school cafeteria and the Biology Department—and proud of my first published stories: an interview with the cafeteria manager and a story on the comparative chest expansions of the football team. Gerhart poked fun at both of these articles.

Because he often worked nights, he had free time during the day. He began to pick me up at school at the beginning of the lunch hour, driving me home for what Mother called "a good hot lunch," which was usually eggs *à la* goldenrod, and delivering me back to school in time for class. At first this seemed convenient. Then I understood that Gerhart's real motive was not my hot lunch but showing boys at school that I was his property.

I began to take my lunch to school once more and to make excuses to prevent Gerhart's coming over in the evening: a paper to write, a French test the next day, poetry to memorize. He came, but he did not come into the house. Mother reported that he often sat in his car parked across the street, watching to see if I stayed home. Mother found his possessiveness both amusing and flattering.

Mother, who once told me I was seeing too much of Gerhart, began to say, "Now, you be nice to Gerhart. He's lonely, and he's been good to you."

Had he been good to me? As Mother pointed out, we saw only movies he wanted to see, never those I wanted to see, not even Katharine Hepburn in *Little Women*. And what about his sulking at losing at two-handed bridge and his continual ridicule of activities I enjoyed? More and more, I did not want to be nice to Gerhart. I edged away from him, sitting as far away from him as I could whenever I went out in his car.

Other boys my age began to appear more interesting.

At school, I had casual, joking friendships with boys, but these were not the boys who asked me to go to school dances or to the movies. Three boys from school did take me out, but they were shy, serious, and awkward. The boys were disappointed in me, too. Away from school, I was shy, serious, and awkward. Inviting them into the house for something to eat did not occur to me, probably because Mother did not suggest it.

A Reed College freshman I shall call Roger, who was introduced to me by a classmate, invited me to a dance held in the Reed College Commons. Roger turned out to be more interesting than high school boys, even though his dancing was worse than mine. He loped to some mysterious rhythm all his own, with great enthusiasm and sweat on his brow.

When he brought me home, he parked his grandmother's Franklin in our driveway and sat with his hands resting on the steering wheel. Finally I asked, "Aren't you going to get out and open the door for me?"

He grinned and said, "That bit of chivalry is outmoded. Women are capable of opening car doors for themselves."

Secretly I agreed, but, having taken a stand, I

felt I could not back down. "I won't get out till you open the door," I informed him.

"And I am not going to open it for you," he said.

I sat and he sat.

Mother, I was sure, would be waiting to lecture me, "What will the neighbors think with you parked in the driveway with a boy until all hours?" I had to find a way out of this impasse, and fast. I finally rolled down the car window and climbed out without opening the door. Roger then got out of the car and walked me up the steps.

For the next couple of years, Roger occasionally took me loping around the floor of the Reed College Commons or the dance floor at Jantzen Beach, an amusement park popular with the high school and college crowd. We never argued about his opening the door again; I opened it myself. Instead, we argued about kissing.

One evening, when Roger brought me home, he asked, "May I kiss you?"

"Of course not," I said. Girls did not kiss boys quite so readily. Besides, I was self-conscious about my mouthful of wire.

"You're overcompensating," Roger said. "You want to kiss me so much you are afraid to."

"That's the dumbest thing I ever heard," I told him in indignation.

If he had kissed me without asking, I doubt

that I would have minded. As it was, we never kissed. We argued. Roger made me realize there were men who were much more interesting to talk to than Gerhart.

Unexpectedly, something happened to take my mind temporarily off boys. Miss Burns, the chairman of the English Department, called me into her office and asked me, as president of the Migwan Club, to take charge of writing the script for the Girls' League Show, which was to raise money for a scholarship. All girls in school automatically belonged to the league. She suggested Jane Welday, a bright girl with a sense of humor, as another writer. The show was to involve as many school clubs as we could work in.

Jane and I concocted a script called *They Had to See Europe*. We worked hard and fast, taking turns writing episodes that involved stereotypical characters: Joan, a debutante, seeing Europe with her father, D. Saunders Clarke, "president of the First National Bank of Scappoose"; Bob, a handsome young chemist in love with Joan; a mother with a spoiled little girl; two comic spinsters; a stowaway poet; and a pair of comic detectives, Oscar MacSnarf and Homer J. Butterbottom. This drama, which involved love and stolen jewels, took place on the deck of a ship represented by a railing with a life preserver in front of the curtain. At the end of each scene, the auditorium would be darkened, the ship's railing hoisted out of sight by the stage crew, and the curtains opened to reveal the travelers in a different country.

When the script was complete, Mrs. Graham, the biology teacher in charge of the production, said to me, "Beverly, you are just as pretty as the girls who get all the attention around this school. Miss Burns and I want you to play the leading lady."

I thought of myself as a plain girl with an unruly permanent wave, no lipstick, and a mouthful of glittering bands and wires, but now—well yes, thank you, Mrs. Graham, I would be delighted to play the leading lady.

As I walked home with Claudine, I was elated. No one had ever called me pretty before. I suddenly felt pretty. Pretty me! Pretty me!

This was one day I did not stop at Claudine's house. I hurried home to tell Mother; I telephoned friends. Mother, as pleased as I, told our next-door neighbor. "Good for you," everyone said. "It's time someone other than the same old clique received some attention."

Just before supper, the telephone rang. I answered. The call was from a girl prominent in Girls' League. Maybe some of the girls were becoming less snobbish, I thought. Then she said, "Some of us have been talking it over and have decided you should drop out of the show."

I had trouble believing what I was hearing.

"How come?" I finally asked, my pleasure turning to bewilderment and then to anger.

"Because you don't have the clothes to play the part," she informed me.

Bolstered by one of Mother's maxims from my childhood, "Show your spunk," I did not agree to withdraw.

This insulting call infuriated Mother. She began to relate the incident by telephone to her friends, always concluding with, "I don't know whether to have her go through with it or not."

Finally I told Mother I had every intention of going through with the show. But how? Fortunately, others rallied in my behalf. Our next-door neighbor offered a Spanish shawl, fringed and embroidered in silk, for an evening wrap to wear over my own bias-cut white satin formal, my one treasured luxury. Virginia, my most prosperous friend, said, "Bev, you can borrow any of my things." Her clothes were made by a dressmaker.

I overheard Mother whisper a surprising statement to Dad: "If she has it in her to go ahead and be somebody, we should back her up." She never made such statements to me.

I was doubtful about borrowing clothes, for Mother had taught me never to borrow anything more than a cup of sugar; but for once, Mother relaxed her anti-borrowing rule. "Virginia is such a good-hearted girl," she said, and I agreed. I selected several dresses, matching, but not quite fitting, shoes, and a coat. Rehearsals, after-school hours of excitement and fun, began. A rumor was started that the boy who was to play the young chemist madly in love with Joan would *really* kiss me as the curtain descended at the end of the show. We both backed away from this during rehearsals.

Mother tried to persuade Gerhart to attend the show, but he refused. I was glad.

The night of the performance, there was a great flurry of being made up (lipstick at last!) by the drama teacher and changing into costumes, everyone busy, important, in a hurry. The houselights were dimmed by the chief of the stage crew, and on the arm of a portly boy billed as D. S. Clarke, my father and president of the Scappoose Bank, I stepped out before the footlights in front of a full house.

The pair of detectives appeared and accused my father of smuggling jewels. Not having expected to play a part in the production, I was stuck with lines such as, "But, Father—"

Bob, the chemist, appeared and cried, "Joan!"

I cried back, "Bob! You shouldn't be here! The only reason Father is taking me to Europe is to get me away from you!"

This drama continued between acts in Germany, France, England, and Italy, where D. S. Clarke and I squatted and scooted across the

287

stage behind a one-dimensional gondola while "Funiculi, Funicula" was played by Grant's one accordion player.

The plot hung on D. S. Clarke's seasickness and some curative pills invented by Bob, which he produced when the president of the First National Bank of Scappoose moaned, "Go away, everybody, and let me die!" After one of Bob's pills, the bank president made an instant recovery and asked the price of the prescription from Bob.

Bob: "Nothing, if you will let me marry Joan."

D. S. Clarke: "Marry her! Young man, you may take her with my blessing."

My last line was "Father!" as I fell into the arms of Bob, who kissed me rather hastily as the curtain was lowered—but that kiss was long enough to let me know that there were better kisses in the world than Gerhart's.

The curtain rose again. Applause. Bows. The eyeglasses of my parents twinkled from the center of the third row. Afterward friends and several boys I barely knew gathered to congratulate me.

The next week I received a formal note from the league thanking me for my contribution.

Pooh to you, I thought.

Employment

Toward the end of my junior year, on a trip to the orthodontist, I detoured into Meier & Frank's personnel office for an application for a summer job as a cashier or elevator operator. Proud of my attempt at helping out and eager for a bit of independence, I told my parents what I had done.

"You are not filling out any application for Meier & Frank," said Dad.

"But I want to help," I protested, near tears.

"No daughter of ours is going to be seen working in Meier & Frank," said Mother.

Everyone was short of money. Mrs. Miles planned to take her girls out to harvest strawberries and raspberries when school was out and invited Claudine and me to go along. Even though I knew the work would be back-breaking,

I was eager to go, to earn money, to be with my friends.

"Certainly not," said Mother.

"Mrs. Klum is letting Claudine go," I persisted.

"I don't care what Mrs. Klum is letting Claudine do," said Mother. "You're not going." Then she added, "I don't see how Mrs. Miles manages with five girls."

Just before school was out, Mother telephoned the dean of girls at Grant to ask if someone in the neighborhood wanted a baby-sitter. I was humiliated. If she wanted me to baby-sit for strangers, why couldn't I ask the dean myself? I received a call from a woman wanting me to stay with her two-year-old son for an afternoon. I did not even know there was a two-year-old in the neighborhood. During the Depression, babies were luxuries few people in our neighborhood could afford. The baby next door, with whom I sat when he was asleep, was the only one I knew. Apprehensively, I went to the woman's house. She pointed to the kitchen stacked with dirty dishes I was to wash, peas to shell, the vacuum cleaner in the middle of the living room, dusting to be done. About her little boy her parting words were "I hope you can do something with him. I can't."

I spent a terrible afternoon. The child was more than I could handle and still cope with housework. As soon as I put my hands in dish-water, he was out the back door and down the street. I ran after him and carried him, kicking and screaming, home. He refused to take his nap. He threw things. He hit me. Somehow I managed to get through the stack of dishes while trying to keep the child from harm. Late in the afternoon I sat down on the kitchen floor with him and enter-tained him by getting him to shell peas along with me while I thought longingly of an elevator at Meier & Frank and a real paycheck, even a small one. At six o'clock the mother came home, frowned at the vacuum cleaner still in the middle of the living room, handed me fifty cents, and told me to vacuum the living room before I left.

I felt incompetent and exploited, and I flatly refused ever again to baby-sit for strangers. This angered Mother. Helping out would not hurt me, she said. I wanted to help, but not by being paid a pittance trying to do two jobs at once in some-one's dirty kitchen.

My junior year ended. Franklin Roosevelt was running for President. "Wouldn't it be wonderful if he were elected and could turn this country around?" Mother said, not really believing he could.

Mother's old friends from her school-teaching days wrote that they were coming to Portland. She replied, "What a disappointment! We have to be out of town just when you are going to be here." We did not answer the telephone while they were in town. "Friends," Mother said, "cost money."

My father spent his vacation painting the outside of the house. I heard worried whispers between my parents. How were they ever going to set anything aside for their old age? What were they going to do with Beverly? I wondered, too. I had no idea what I was going to do with myself.

Once Gerhart, in spite of Mother's disapproval, took me to see a marathon dance contest. Those pathetic, exhausted couples dragging one another around the dance floor under the supervision of a smarmy master of ceremonies in hopes of winning a few dollars—and what about the losers? They were desperate, too. This was the Depression at its most degrading. I demanded to be taken home, away from those hurting, shuffling feet.

When Gerhart said he wanted to buy one of the new Ford V-8s, Mother said, "Now, Gerhart, don't you do it. You save your money. You'll need it someday." As he drove up the driveway in a new V-8, I had an irrational feeling of surprise that he had defied Mother, and a taste of bitterness because he could afford a new car when Dad had been forced to sell ours.

Then Claudine and her mother left for Puddin',

and Gerhart drove off to California to spend his two weeks' vacation visiting his family. I was glad to see him go, so very glad I went limp with relief and faced at last how much I had come to dislike him.

When the Fourth of July came, Mother said, "You should have an invitation to a picnic. When I was your age, boys always invited me to Fourth of July picnics, and we always had a glorious time."

Even though I felt guilty, a social failure and disappointment to my mother, I did not want to go to a Fourth of July picnic. I wanted a real job, or I wanted to be left alone to lie on my bed in my room and read Willa Cather.

My reading, secluded in my room with the door shut, annoyed Mother. She constantly talked to me through the door and accused me of being snooty. I was not snooty. I was confused and unhappy, and wanted time to think without Mother telling me what to think.

One afternoon, when Gerhart had been gone about a week, I was lying on my bed watching butterflies sip from purple panicles of sun-warmed blossoms on the bush outside my window, and wondering what was to become of me, when Mother called from the dining room, "Beverly, come here a minute."

As I stepped from the hall door into the living

room, a hand reached out and stroked my hair. It was Gerhart, who had flattened himself against the wall so I would not see him until I was in the room. I was startled and angry, cheated out of another week without him.

"Come on. Let's go for a ride," he said, or ordered, for Mother was sure to say, "Go on, Beverly. You've been cooped up all day."

We drove around awhile, ending in the usual place, the Swan Island airport, where Gerhart turned to me and said, "Will you marry me?"

Marry him? Marriage to anyone, especially Gerhart, was of no interest to me when my life had not really begun. Embarrassed and bewildered, I made my refusal as tactful as I could manage. A proposal of marriage was, after all, supposed to be the greatest compliment a man could pay. Gerhart's jaw clenched. He shoved his V-8 into gear and, without a word, drove me home and left. Mother gave me a sharp look, but I said nothing.

Gerhart did not stay away. I resented his touching me and shrugged away from him. Once, when his grasp was insistent, I startled him by ordering, "Unhand me, greybeard loon!" He obeyed, but must have been mystified by the words from "The Rime of the Ancient Mariner." He had not been required to memorize hundreds of lines of poetry.

One evening, when my father and I were alone in the living room, Dad said quietly, "You know, you don't have to go out with Gerhart if you don't want to." I don't remember my answer, but I do remember how his gentle words soothed my troubled heart. I knew I had an ally in what had become an intolerable situation, one that was abetted by Mother. Why, when she was so quick to point out Gerhart's flaws to me? I can only guess that my life made her life more interesting, she was trying to relive her youth through me, and she enjoyed her duties as self-appointed chaperone on picnics and trips to the beach.

It was Claudine who unknowingly rescued me. She wrote from Puddin' inviting me to come out for a while.

I was packed and was waiting when Mr. Klum picked me up in his gray Model T sedan, to which he was fiercely loyal because "it gets me where I want to go." With Spud, a dog he had rescued from the pound for company when he worked nights, we drove out of Portland through Oregon City, turned off the highway at a water tank, wound past meadows of grazing cows, drove through a covered bridge, and on until we came to the Colvins' Pudding River Camp Ground and Picnic Resort and the Klums' cabin, which Mr. Klum called "the shack" in the same affectionate way he called Spud his "pooch."

Puddin'

The Colvin family's campground was located on the lower part of a farm that had been in the Colvin family for several generations. Cows grazed beside the Pudding River, and in the center of the meadow was a roofed dance floor open at the sides and lined with built-in benches. Three families had built simple one-room cabins in a grove of Douglas fir trees, while others pitched tents, some for pleasure, others for shelter, while they earned money picking beans that grew on a plot of land at the bottom of the hill. At the top of the hill were fields of grain and the original farmhouse, probably as old as the house we had once owned in Yamhill.

Claudine and I carried water in a five-gallon can from the little store near the dance floor. The water sloshed and splashed, catching the sunlight and tossing it back like the reflection from a crazy mirror. We split kindling for the wood stove, or more often, when we saw a boy approach, Claudine picked up the hatchet and chopped inefficiently. The boy always stopped to help. We walked to public rest rooms near the dressing rooms, in a building made entirely of old doors.

We ate our meals out under the firs on a table that was Mr. Klum's pride, a table made of a cross section of a fir tree set on a stump. This tree had been between four and five hundred years old when it was felled. Claudine and I never finished counting the rings, but we did mark a few important years—the year we were born, the years of the World War.

While we ate, Spud chased chipmunks. Once Claudine remarked, "Spud is a chippy chaser." Mr. Klum laughed.

"Why, Claudine," said her mother, "don't ever let me hear you use that word again."

"What word?" asked Claudine, surprised.

"That word you just said," said Mrs. Klum. "Just don't say it again."

Claudine and I, baffled and amused, called chipmunks chippies whenever her mother was out of earshot. We learned the meaning later when I asked Mother, who answered primly, "a chippy is a woman who sells her body." How does she do that? I wondered but did not ask. Something about Mother's manner prevented me.

Early Sunday morning, picnickers, a good cash crop for the Colvins, began to arrive, paying twenty-five cents a car, eager to establish with boxes and baskets territorial rights to the best tables and outdoor stoves. Puddin' was a place of picnics: family picnics, church picnics, club picnics, lodge picnics. Children yelled and raced, babies cried, dogs barked and sometimes fought, women talked as they laid tables and set out food. From the river came the *thwump* of the diving board, shouts and splashes. The clang of metal against metal rang in our ears as men pitched horseshoes. Children played chopsticks on the out-of-tune piano on the dance floor, bats thwacked against softballs, picnickers cheered. Woodsmoke wafted through the trees. "Smoke follows beauty" was said to any girl who fanned it away from her face.

The farm food! Fried chicken, baked ham, potato salad, meat loaf and scalloped potatoes, green beans simmered with bacon, freshly picked corn, homemade chowchow and piccalilli, fruit salad with whipped cream dressing, coleslaw made with real sour cream, cucumbers floating in vinegar, sliced tomatoes that had ripened on the vine, pies, cakes and cookies, freezers of homemade ice cream made with thick farm cream, watermelons that sounded hollow when thumped and were carried to the river to cool.

An hour, a very long hour after eating—swimming, splashing, pushing one another off the float, lying in the sun on wood bleached by weather while children raced and sometimes shouted, "Look! I'm leaving footprints in the sands of time!" Then a meal of leftovers before gathering at the dance floor, where the crowd sat on the benches along the sides. Older boys, if they could spare a nickel, hung around under the trees drinking Orange Crush or Green River out of the bottles. One of the Colvins grated paraffin on the floor to smooth it for dancing. Little boys ran and skidded.

"Come on, Claudine, play something," someone called out.

Claudine obligingly went to the piano and played whatever popular tune came into her head: "Goofus," "Bye Bye Blackbird," "Me and My Shadow." A few young people got up to dance. Children tried to dance, giggled, tripped, and ran off. Extra girls sat on the sidelines trying not to look wistful, gave up, and danced with one another. We all hoped to dance with Bobby Colvin, tan and muscular from farm work and filled with exuberance lacking in city boys during the Depression.

Finally a weary old sedan pulled up beside the dance floor. "Now we can begin!" someone shouted as a woman and two men climbed out. Claudine tactfully left the piano.

One man carried a saxophone; the other lugged a set of drums up the steps and set it beside the piano. The woman carried a box, which she set in front of the drums. On the front of the box was a crudely painted face of a cat with a hole for its open mouth. The woman smoothed her freshly washed percale dress beneath her and, with knobby work-reddened hands, struck a chord to capture attention.

"Folks," announced the drummer, "don't forget to feed Kitty. He's mighty hungry tonight."

One of the Colvin brothers fumbled in the pocket of his overalls for a quarter to drop into the cat's mouth. Children gasped. A whole quarter! The drums thumped, the saxophone bleated, and the worn hammers of the piano beat against the strings. "Let Me Call You Sweetheart." A waltz. Young people were disappointed, their parents and grandparents brightened, and men muttered, "Well, I guess I might as well . . ." as they took the hands of partners. Children didn't care about the music. They grabbed one another and pranced around the floor.

When the piano player plunked out "Shave and

a haircut, two bits" to mark the end of a number, the drummer shouted, "Kitty's hungry!"

An embarrassing pause followed as everyone hoped someone else would feed Kitty. Finally someone dug a nickel or a dime out of a pocket, Kitty was fed, and music continued: a fox-trot, a schottische, or a polka. Faces grew flushed, skin was cooled by the night air as mist rose from the river. Young people, who considered the dances old-fashioned, drifted over to the store for Cokes bought with nickels they had earned picking beans.

Dancing ended early. Farmers who had to get up to milk cows needed their rest. City picnickers had the long drive—over twenty miles—into Portland.

Mrs. Klum led the way back to the cabin with a flashlight, and Claudine and I climbed into bed on the porch, where we were weighed down by the heavy homemade quilts. Her head rested on a red felt canoe pillow with "Stella" in white letters; my head rested on a softer pillow embroidered with a branch of pepper berries and the words "I love you, California." Overhead, through the fir trees, we could hear the drone of the ten o'clock mail plane from California. When a train whistled, Claudine named the musical notes of the whistle. I fell asleep thinking of those work-worn hands playing "Let Me Call You Sweetheart" for nickels and dimes on a broken-down piano.

Weekdays at Puddin' were lazy and peaceful. Mrs. Klum pottered about, transplanting sword ferns to the rotting centers of fir stumps around the cabin.

Mr. Klum felt that his dog would appreciate an outdoor vacation, so Spud was left behind when he returned to Portland for the week. Claudine and I took Spud for walks around the campground along a wagon road, past a field of dense tepees of green beans and through a woodsy canyon up the hill to the old farmhouse to watch harvesters.

After lunch I knitted while Claudine read aloud from Sigrid Undset's *Kristin Lavransdatter,* and when the necessary wait of an hour had passed, we wiggled, complaining, into our woolen bathing suits damp from the day before and walked down to the river to swim and to wash. We sometimes had to swim after the floating soap as the current carried it downstream. Afterward Claudine and I lay on the raft, where the sun warmed us, pressing us against the weathered silver boards. Portland and Gerhart seemed a long way away.

The next weekend, Mother sent word by Mr. Klum that I should return with him on Sunday evening. My Great-aunt Elizabeth was coming from California to visit. I was sorry, very sorry, to leave.

Sunday evening, when Mr. Klum left me at the foot of our driveway, I felt serene, sun-tinged, and happy.

Mother's first words were "Beverly! You've ruined your complexion!"

I flopped into the nearest chair. "Mother," I said, pleading and without anger, "it does seem as if no matter what I do, you make me feel guilty."

"Why, that's ridiculous," she said.

Somehow I found the courage to contradict. "No, it isn't ridiculous. You do make me feel guilty," I insisted, still without anger. I wanted so much to talk honestly with Mother, to tell her my feelings, to become her friend.

Mother stiffened, her mouth a straight line. "Well, excuse me for living," she said.

For the first time, I understood that I was afraid of Mother for the guilt she made me bear, and that I could never have an honest conversation with her. The woman I wanted for a friend would always be right; I would always be wrong. I have never understood why, for Mother was genuinely kind to others and could be kind to me when I did exactly as she wished.

Then Great-aunt Elizabeth, the mother of the two young teachers Mother had accompanied out

West in her youth, came to visit from Southern California, where she lived in turn with her daughters. She was tiny, vivacious, and talkative, loved pretty clothes, and had about her an aura of lightheartedness. She seemed unaware of the Depression, and in her company Mother became the person I remembered from childhood.

Great-aunt Elizabeth seemed to confirm what most of my high school class believed: that everything good in life existed in California. We had learned from the radio and from postcards that in California the sun shone all year round on trees, in groves instead of orchards, heavy with oranges. Highways were lined with wildflowers more vivid than Oregon's wildflowers. Instead of farming and logging in the rain, Californians made movies in the sunshine. Life in California was one long, happy fiesta with everyone dancin' with Anson at the Mark Hopkins, dancing at the Avalon Ballroom on Catalina Island, and dining in a restaurant shaped like a derby. We knew all this was fantasy, but still—somehow, someplace, life had to be better than Portland, Oregon, in the 1930s.

My great-aunt, with her lively chatter and frivolous ways, brightened our lives for a few days. When we saw her off on a Princess ship for California, I was sorry to see her go.

The Happiest Days

Our senior year in high school, neighbors said to Claudine and me, "Don't forget, these are the happiest days of your life." Others hinted at the possibility of a June wedding for Beverly. Mother, who enjoyed keeping neighbors guessing, answered with an arch smile, "We'll see." On the surface, our lives must have appeared serene. Mother was careful about that.

But things were not serene in our household. Dad disliked his job in "that hole," as he called his office by the steel door of the bank vault. He was now in his mid-forties, too old to find another job during the Depression, worried about my education and about putting money away for old age. I felt as if he were serving a sentence, condemned to support Mother and me. I was bitter and felt

305

Dad must be, too, because Gerhart, whose only responsibility was payments on his new V-8, earned the same salary.

Mother was tense and apprehensive. I continued to overhear shreds of anxious conversation about my future.

What future, I wondered, and why couldn't my parents speak directly to me about it? I wanted to write; writing was expected of me, but what did I, an ordinary girl, have to write about? I could not depend on my pen and imagination for a living. I visualized nothing beyond, perhaps, business school and a dull office job—if I could find one, and I did not want to find one. An office meant one thing: typewriting.

Claudine and I made sardonic jokes about being lovely girls who would someday make good wives, which meant washing on Monday, ironing on Tuesday, and all the rest of our mothers' routines. I supposed that someday I would become someone's good wife, but never, never Gerhart's.

About that time, Gerhart surprised us by announcing he had joined Jehovah's Witnesses. Any possibility of war or disaster brought him smiling to our door. *This* might be the beginning of the Battle of Armageddon, when Witnesses would be saved and the rest of us would perish. For once Mother and I were united; we could not accept such a negative philosophy. Mother, who enjoyed a good argument, often challenged Gerhart on the subject of Witnesses while I tried to study in the breakfast nook.

Some of my friends began to give parties in their homes, to which I was invited, and Gerhart, too, even though others were not separated into couples. He was contemptuous of these innocent parties, as he was of all my high school activities; but he always went, even though he disliked dancing and often had deep circles under his eyes from having worked a night shift.

We danced to radio music, telephoning announcers with requests for records to be played: "My Blue Heaven," "Willow, Weep for Me," "Pennies from Heaven," and my favorite, "You're Going to Lose Your Gal." A high point of the evening, in addition to supper prepared by a mother, was requesting "The Daring Young Man on the Flying Trapeze," dedicated to someone at the party. If it was actually played, we sang along with the radio, feeling we were having a hilarious time. Boys who were at a loss for conversation said "Wanna buy a duck?"—a phrase picked up from Joe Penner, a radio comedian.

Mother arranged parties for me and planned food, prepared with my assistance. Dad worked hard, too, rolling up the rugs on Saturday afternoon and polishing the Siberian oak floors, and on Sunday, after they had been danced on, repolishing them. My parties were always successful, but somehow I felt that Mother, in spite of the extra work, enjoyed them more than I and that they were really her parties.

That winter, Prohibition ended. Not even Mother's willpower had been able to prevent it. Our lives went on as usual. Roger asked me to go out; I accepted. We went dancing, or loping, at Jantzen Beach, where the crowd gathered around the bandstand when a musician in a yellow jacket set aside his saxophone to take the microphone and sing

> *All night long the rain drops tinkle,*
> *Do you think a little drink'll*
> *Do us any harm?*

That the song referred to alcohol did not occur to me because I had never seen anyone drink so much as a beer. I was, however, fascinated with rhyming "tinkle" and "drink'll."

Whenever I went to a party, Mother insisted on talking it over the next morning. Feeling guilty because I had not enjoyed myself more, I did the best I could with my account, and sometimes we shared genuine laughter. She then passed it all on to her friends, with embellishments. "Oh my, yes, Beverly had a glorious time and didn't get home until midnight. She had us worried there for a while." One day when I came home from school and laid my books on the dining room table, I picked up a composition book that I thought was Mother's household budget. Instead, it was a diary, not of Mother's life, but of mine, recorded by Mother.

"Mother!" I said, shocked.

"You mind your own business!" she said, snatching the composition book from me.

I could not answer. My life was my business, I thought—or it should be! I never saw the diary again or mentioned it to Mother. What was the use? Whatever I said would be wrong, but I wondered, since Mother said she wanted to write, why she didn't write stories instead of her version of my life.

After that I began to keep a diary of my own in an effort to convince myself that everything was as it should be. That diary is a record of little parties, of amusing incidents at school. Frequently I recorded that Gerhart bored me stiff.

Then a neighborhood boy, whom I shall call Gene, a Reed College student, took me to several school dances and a school play. He was a nice-looking, intelligent boy, serious, and not particularly interesting to me. However, I liked him because he was not Gerhart and because he had gone to Grant, which gave us a foundation for conversation.

For some reason, my going out with Gene upset my parents, who accused me of running after him. Mother said he asked me to go to the school play in return for an invitation to my party.

As I reread my old diary, both on and between the lines, I am puzzled about why they felt this way.

When Claudine, Lorraine, and Olive, members of Job's Daughters, suggested I invite a boy to a dance at the Masonic Hall, I asked Gene, who had taken me to a high school dance. He accepted, and I included him in a party at my house. I was too shy with boys to do much pursuing, and in those days telephoning a boy was considered improper. He initiated the friendship, not I, but I did hope he would telephone. My diary records my worries that he might not actually appear to take me to the class play because he had asked me so far ahead; but he did appear, and we enjoyed a pleasant evening. He also invited me to a couple of Reed College dances. He gave me my first corsage and a box of candy.

Real anger, honest anger, burst through on one page of that diary, probably the only completely honest page written that year. I wrote, in the heat of indignation and with a disregard for the rules of punctuation, "Oh, Hades! I don't want to go to Grant's party with Gerhart and my parents know it. Of course they had to start out on a dissertation on my liking Gene and Mother had to talk about how badly she felt about Gerhart and all that and said that after my next party she was going to tell him not to come back any more. Well, darn it! I don't care. I don't see why she can't see that I'm positively so sick of him I could scream when I even see him. I think Dad backs me up, too. She says I'm selfish and tactless, but how can she expect me to know how to act whenever anyone calls up she listens to every word and prompts me at regular intervals and when I go anyplace she gives me a lecture on what to do and say and think and eat. When I give a party *she* has me give a party and it's the same way with everything."

Why? Wanting to go out with a different boy seems normal, not selfish. And why did Mother feel that telling Gerhart not to come back was her right, not mine? An only daughter of a possessive mother develops a kind of selfishness in a struggle to preserve something of herself, something that does not belong to her mother, but this is a mother-daughter problem that has little to do with boys. Tactless? Yes, I was tactless, even unkind, to Gerhart because I was beyond caring what he thought. I wanted him to give up and go away forever. To me, Gene was only a relief from Gerhart.

And then one day as I was walking home from

school, Gene's mother, smiling and friendly, called me across the street and said, "Saturday is Gene's birthday," and added in the voice of one bestowing an honor, "I am giving a surprise party for him, and *you* are invited." Then her smile changed as she lowered her voice, confiding an exciting secret: "Gene has a girl!" Even though I had never thought of myself as Gene's girl, I was stunned and politely refused the invitation. I was going to be busy Saturday evening, I said.

Mother was furious, when I told her, at this pointed rejection of her daughter. Dad said little, but I knew he was angry, too. I felt even more depressed, for at the time it seemed to me that Gene's mother must feel that I was a girl who, unlike her son, had no future. In later years I wondered if perhaps she thought my relationship with a young man six years older than I had been more intimate than it actually was and that I might be a bad influence on her son. Mother, who had always said, "A girl's most valuable possession is her good name," should have understood.

After that episode, I no longer wanted to go to parties but went, trying to avoid Gerhart by going with one of the girls whose father was driving her. Once when Gerhart had to arrive late because of his working hours, Mother informed me I must let him bring me home. If I did not, she would call off the party she was "having" me give. The guests had been invited, so I complied.

That Sunday after my own party, when Gerhart telephoned, I said, "Please don't come back. I don't want to see you again." I felt heavy and exhausted as I spoke.

Gerhart, calling from the private home where he rented a room, answered in a tight voice, "Are you sure?"

"Yes."

"That is quite all right," he said. I knew he was having trouble sounding casual, as if nothing were wrong, for the benefit of the family he lived with.

At first I experienced the debilitating fatigue that follows the end of an emotional ordeal. I wanted to sleep or sit staring out the window. This was followed by light-hearted relief. My hurt by Gene's mother did not cut very deep; her son was not that important to me. I did not care if I never went to another high school party. I did not care if I could not live up to Mother's expectations of popularity. I did not care what the neighbors thought when they no longer saw cars parked in our driveway.

At first Mother said sadly, "Well, if that's the way you really feel about him . . ." Of course it was. I had been trying to tell her for months. She passed on the news to her friends.

I had such trouble concentrating on my studies that in addition to keeping a diary, I began to write to pen pals I had acquired through Camp Fire Girls, an organization I had dropped. I wrote to the girl in Minnesota and to the English girl, who passed my name on to a boy in Accra on the Gold Coast (now Ghana) of Africa. Through my French class, I began to write in laborious French, with the copious use of *n'est-ce pas,* to a girl in Paris.

These pen pals made Mother nervous. "Never write in a letter anything you aren't willing to see on the front page of a newspaper," she advised. She also worried, "What if these people come to Portland and expect us to put them up?" In Oregon, fruits, vegetables, and out-of-town people were "put up."

I wrote on and on. The girl in Minnesota, with her tales of parties, tap-dancing, and canoeing, was probably trying to create the same happy-American-girl stereotype I was striving for in silly letters I was writing her.

When the boy in Africa sent me half the skin of a small animal with long, glossy black hair, which Dad thought must be a monkey skin, Mother was horrified. "It might attract moths," she said.

I refused to throw the skin away, wrapped it in tissue paper, and hid it in a drawer. In writing to my pen pals, I was trying to reach out to a wider world beyond northeast Portland, Oregon, where, in those Depression days, travel was a trip to the coast or, for the prosperous, a trip to California. That furred skin somehow was proof that, as geography books said, the world was large and full of many different people.

Then Mother began to say she missed Gerhart. She wished he would come over to see *her*. He did come, I suspect because she invited him. Grimly I cloistered myself in the breakfast nook with diary, notepaper, and a pile of books and refused to come out. Gerhart invented excuses for coming over—he needed to use my typewriter; he wanted to bring Mother a magazine. I refused to see him.

Finally Mother, over my objections, invited him to Christmas dinner. "Poor Gerhart," she said. "I don't like to think of him eating Christmas dinner alone in a restaurant."

When Gerhart arrived, Mother, busy in the kitchen, sent me to open the door for him. He had brought a sprig of mistletoe, which he held over my head. "I get a kiss!" he said.

I backed away. "No you don't!"

He grabbed me hard with one arm while holding the mistletoe over my head with his other hand. I fought, and fought with all my strength. I wanted to cry out to my father, sitting in the corner of the dining room, but I was afraid to.

My father was a strong man with heavy fists, who, although he did not say so to me, disliked Gerhart. Gerhart dropped the mistletoe and, with the strength of both his arms, forced his kiss on me. I no longer disliked him. I despised him.

Dinner was miserable for all of us. Gerhart sat in sullen silence and, when he did speak, talked of Jehovah's Witnesses. I was too angry to talk. Afterward Mother complained that Gerhart had ruined her day, and after she had worked so hard to prepare a nice dinner, too.

I spent the rest of Christmas vacation on a required essay to be entered in the Gorgas Memorial Essay Contest. The subject was "The Past Benefits and Future Importance to Man of the Control of Disease-bearing Mosquitoes." I resented every word of it.

Still Gerhart persisted in coming to our house. I remained in the breakfast nook, toiling over *Practice Leaves in English,* the only workbook we used in twelve years in the public schools. Because senior English was the year of the essay, I labored over such topics as "Macbeth's Worst Enemy" and "Could Beowulf Make the Team?"

Teachers were concerned about me. One of my former biology teachers hired me to grade papers and, when she paid me, always said, "This is for your college fund." My sociology teacher, after I handed in an interview with Virginia's father (who worked for a lumber company) on communism, labor problems, and company unions in the lumber industry, told me I *must* go to college. Mr. Bittner, the principal, sent me with a group of students "representative of Grant" to spend a day at Oregon State College.

The afternoon I came home from school and discovered my monkey skin was missing from my drawer, I exploded into a confrontation with Mother. "Where is it?" I demanded. "What did you do with my monkey skin?"

Mother remained calm and righteous. "I threw it in the garbage," she said. "I didn't want it in the house."

"It was beautiful, and it was *my* monkey skin!" I stormed. "You had no right to throw it away. You had no right to go through my drawers!"

"I didn't want it in my house," repeated Mother, undismayed by my anger, "and you needn't look at me like that!"

Her house. Why didn't she say "our house"? Years of pent-up anger roiled within me, but as always I felt hopeless. I said no more about the monkey skin.

For the first time, my grades dropped to straight G's instead of the usual mixture of E's and G's. "Mother and Dad aren't going to like this," I said, showing my report card to Claudine.

Lucky Claudine. Her parents felt her grades were her business, not theirs.

"Tell them now," advised Claudine. "Maybe they will forget by the weekend."

Mother would not forget, I knew, until I brought my grades up during the next quarter.

Elizabeth Brown peeks between the ears of her horse at the Mount Hood Country Club. Riding in gym bloomers rather than breeches is hard on my bare legs, but I had no choice, as Father is without a job.

BELOW: Ulysses S. Grant High School.
> "U.S. Grant, our school of honored name.
> Goes triumphant on the march to fame.
> We'll raise our banners high.
> We'll hoist them to the sky.
> We're proud of our U.S. Grant.
> Rah! Rah! Rah!"

This is the school song, as remembered by Claudine. We aren't sure about "hoist" but agree that if it isn't the correct word, it should be.

RIGHT: Lucy Grow, our kind and feisty Camp Fire leader, is snapped on her front steps, surrounded by Pukwudjies.

ABOVE: Snapping this awkward picture of me as I try to climb a sandy bank is Gerhart's idea of a joke.

RIGHT: Claudine and I clown at Puddin' while we hope some young man, preferably handsome, will offer to split kindling for us.

Father sits in our backyard beside an arch of Dorothy Perkins roses, proof that Portland is indeed the City of Roses.

ABOVE: I show off my fourteen-dollar graduation dress from Meier & Frank's basement.

RIGHT: I am photographed in Mother's dress for Grant's yearbook, Memoirs, *whose dedication, written by Jane Elton, fellow Migwan, reads: "To Life . . . with its winding bewildering roads . . . to the world with its joys and burdensome loads. . . . They're ours to learn . . . to take and give. May fortune be with us in learning to live."*

A Letter

Outside our house, by the front door, was a mail slot that led to a metal chute about a foot long that ended with a little door in the living room. Although mail was delivered twice a day, Mother opened the little door half a dozen times, feeling inside the chute in case a letter got stuck. "I'm going to have to get after that mailman," she always said when the mailbox was empty.

One day, Mother pulled out a letter from Great-aunt Elizabeth's daughter Verna, who was the librarian at Chaffey High School and Junior College in Ontario, in Southern California. First Mother admired, as she always did, Verna's beautiful upright "librarian's hand," the handwriting taught for writing catalog cards before typewriters were commonly used in libraries.

Then Mother opened and read the letter. She appeared to reread it before she tucked it back in the envelope and tossed it aside with a little laugh. "Well, if that isn't just like Verna," she said. "She always was impractical."

"How come?" I wanted to know.

"She wants you to come down and spend the next winter going to junior college and living with her family." Verna, I knew, was married to the high school physical education teacher and had a son and daughter younger than I. They also owned an orange grove. The letter said California junior colleges did not charge tuition.

This invitation seemed as impractical as an invitation to Never-never Land. I did not take it seriously. That evening, when I had finished supper, Mother read the letter to my father over their tea. "Verna always did have her head in the clouds," I heard her say. "She thinks all Beverly would have to do is get on a boat in Portland and get off in San Pedro, where they would meet her." I did not hear my father reply.

The incident did not seem worth mentioning to Gerhart when he turned up that evening. Prodded by Mother, who would not let me forget how much she missed him, going out with him finally seemed easier than remaining imprisoned in the breakfast nook. At least I would get to go to the movies. We made little effort at conversation but sat through many double features at neighborhood theaters, all recorded in my diary: *Havana Widows* and *Son of a Sailor; I Am Suzanne* and *Hell and High Water; Broadway to Hollywood* and *Before Dawn; She-Wolf of Wall Street* and *Love Birds.*

One evening Gerhart asked me to go for a ride with him because he had to deliver a message for Jehovah's Witnesses. "No thanks," I said. I wanted nothing to do with his church activities.

Mother said, "Now, Beverly, you go along and keep Gerhart company."

So I went, rather than argue. We drove to a house in a suburb of Portland, where Gerhart told me to wait in the car while he went to the door. When he rang the doorbell, a porch light was turned on, a woman opened the door, called the dog, and shouted at Gerhart, "Get the hell out of here! Get off my property and stop trying to break up my home!"

Gerhart ran, jumped into the car, and we sped off. He was so embarrassed he took me to see *Design for Living* and *Orient Express.*

Mother found this episode so funny she wanted me to go to church with Gerhart to find out what it was like. I refused, and recorded in my diary: "My mother is so annoyed with me because I resent her trying to make me go to church with Gerhart that she is loath to speak to me." Eventually, of course, I was worn down and went to a meeting, which was held in someone's backyard by a group of people who seemed so defeated by the Depression that their only hope was the destruction of the world. It was a sad afternoon.

Monday I was glad to return to school, even though, in spite of the interested concern of my teachers, Grant was now a less happy place for me. Teachers had begun to remind us that our college professors would not spoon-feed us like our high school teachers. Girls going to the University of Oregon or Oregon State were looking forward to pre-rushing, rushing, sorority life, a life that seemed to be an extension of Grant's snobbishness—and for catching husbands. Claudine's parents decided she should go to the State Teachers' College in Monmouth where, after two years' study, she would be qualified to teach in the elementary schools of Oregon. Nothing was said about further musical education. Bright boys, those whose parents could afford it, were going to Stanford. Others with good grades were going to Reed College. Some were going to small religious colleges.

I seemed to be the only person at Grant with no plans and no place to go, although I knew this was not true. We were not the only family having a hard time. The Miles family was struggling, too. Lorraine, who had taken typing and short-hand, had graduated from Grant and was learning office work at the Red Cross. Her sisters were finding whatever odd jobs they could.

Mother said over and over, "It does seem as if Oregon does nothing to help its young people." In those days before community colleges, she was right. She felt especially sad for Lorraine, who had won a scholarship to Reed College but was unable to accept because she did not have forty dollars for the late registration fee. Mother said Lorraine was such a bright girl, she wished she had the forty dollars to give her. Lorraine would not have dreamed of asking her family for money, any more than I would have asked my family. Times were too hard.

Then a second letter dropped through our mail slot, a letter for me from Reed College telling me I was eligible for admission and enclosing a scholarship application. (Was Mother behind this letter? I have often wondered.) Under duress, I filled out the application, probably badly, for if there was one place I did not want to go, it was Reed College, no matter how fine its reputation. The thought of living at home, being carsick on the bus twice a day, and studying in the breakfast nook with Gerhart lurking in the living room was intolerable. I heard nothing more from Reed College.

Mother said, "Your father and I cannot leave you money, but we will somehow manage to leave you able to take care of yourself." How? How were they going to do this? What more sacrifices would they have to make, I wondered, and would Mother sacrifice out of love or duty?

Gerhart announced that he was using his vacation to drive to California for a Jehovah's Witnesses conference and taking with him, according to my diary, "a Frenchman and two Greek bootblacks." Good, I thought. I hope California swallows him up.

Even with Gerhart gone, I continued to spend my evenings—those I did not spend at Claudine's house—in the breakfast nook, writing letters to pen pals, recording my days in a diary of no literary value, which I hoped I kept hidden from Mother, and studying. My teeth ached constantly from the tightening of wires.

From the living room I caught the sound of my parents talking quietly, earnestly, in voices they used when talking about me but when they did not want me to hear. Naturally, I laid down my pen to listen. I felt like a burden, a problem, a nuisance.

"But, Lloyd—" I heard my mother protest one evening.

Dad's answer was so soft I could not hear.

Then Mother said, as if in despair, "All right. If you insist."

What was Dad insisting? He rarely insisted. After a long silence, Mother called, "Beverly, come here a minute."

Reluctantly I entered the living room and stood facing my parents. Mother said, "Daddy says you are going to California next winter, staying with Verna, and going to junior college."

This was so different from what I expected, I felt as if lightning had shot through me. I looked to my father for confirmation.

He removed his pipe from his mouth. "I mean it," he said.

"Do you want to go?" Mother asked, obviously hoping I would not.

Finding it hard to believe Mother would let me have a choice, but with Dad in the room to support me, I answered, "Yes. Yes, of course I want to go."

"Well then, I guess that settles it." Mother's voice was so heavy with sorrow I immediately felt guilty. "I better write to Verna," she said, and added the words she spoke so often: "If only Oregon would do something to help its young people."

Back in the breakfast nook, I stared at the cupboards in confusion and disbelief.

After that, there was less antagonism between

Mother and me. She was caught up in this new phase of my life. "Yes, Beverly has been invited to spend the winter in California and go to college." "Yes, I know it's a long way for her to go, but all she has to do is take a boat right here in Portland, and my cousins will meet her in San Pedro." She enjoyed her project, getting me ready for college, even though she was ambivalent about my leaving. "We'll take it one year at a time," she said.

Life moved quickly after that, although in March, when Long Beach was struck by an earthquake, Mother felt I should give up going to California and stay safe in Portland, where the earth did not shake, nor the buildings fall down. Dad and I overruled her. Earthquakes, preferable to the Battle of Armageddon, no longer frightened me. Letters flew back and forth between Portland and Ontario. Clothes were not important at Chaffey—cotton dresses would do. My duties would be keeping my room clean and baking two cakes a week for the family. "Verna always did have a sweet tooth," Mother said.

Dr. Meaney, after I had worn bands for five years, concluded that I had too many teeth for the size of my mouth. One tooth was pulled and my wires tightened once more, but somehow my teeth did not ache as much as they had for the past five and a half years. I had hope.

My grades improved. The dramatics class Mother had objected to so strenuously was fun. For my dramatic monologue, I chose "Patterns," by Amy Lowell, a long poem that Miss Churchill, my former Latin teacher doubling in dramatics, said would be difficult to present. I was eager for a challenge.

This poem felt compatible because I, too, had been "held rigid to a pattern," and quite long enough. Today, as I reread the poem, I marvel at my courage in giving it in front of a high school class—all that tossing off of clothes, running "pink and silver" along the paths while my lover "stumbled after." And those lines about waistcoat buttons bruising "as he clasped me, aching, melting, unafraid—"

"Wow!" said Claudine when I rehearsed "Patterns" for her. "You're sure brave."

For her class she had chosen "Little Boy Blue," by Eugene Field, because it was easy: "The little toy dog is covered with dust, / But sturdy and staunch he stands," and so on. Nobody would laugh at Claudine. Probably no one would listen.

When time came to give my monologue, my courage sagged, but I somehow stepped out of myself as I walked onto the stage, faced the class, and began: "I walk down the garden paths . . ." No one laughed; they listened, and I finished with tears in my eyes and a break in my voice.

I had enough pent-up anguish to carry me through any number of renditions of "Patterns." Miss Churchill praised my performance. Claudine reported she also told her other class what a fine piece of work I had done. That small triumph gave me confidence. With one year of college ahead of me, I studied harder. My improved grades excused me from taking final examinations, which made me feel lighthearted with freedom.

Then the longshoremen struck. No ships were sailing to California.

"That takes care of that," said Mother. "Trains are too expensive."

Dad smoked his pipe awhile before he said, "She can go by Greyhound bus."

Mother was horrified. "Go all that distance by bus? She would have to change buses in San Francisco and in Los Angeles, and they are big cities."

Dad was calm. "If she doesn't have any sense now, she never will have," he said. "She can manage a bus trip."

Mother was dubious. She produced Greyhound schedules to prove her point. Twenty-four hours to San Francisco, another full day to Los Angeles, a short ride to Ontario.

"I'll go if I have to walk," I said with such determination Mother was taken aback. Inwardly I was uneasy. I had seen big cities, full of gangsters, chorus girls, and nightclubs, in the movies, but I had never been much more than a hundred miles from home. To me, Portland was a big city.

Mother wrote to former neighbors who had emigrated to California. A Hancock Street friend would be happy to meet me in San Francisco and also invited me to stay a couple of nights so I could see the city. Another agreed to meet me in Los Angeles, put me up overnight, and see that I caught the right bus to Ontario. It was settled.

Claudine and I, both wearing dark dresses with white collars, went off to have our class pictures taken. Mother advised us, "Always wear white next to your face when you have your picture taken. White reflects light on the face." I wore Mother's best dress, the only dress in the house with a white collar.

The class ordered and sent out our graduation announcements. Presents arrived: several one-dollar bills from neighbors, stationery ("So you'll be sure to write"), panties, stockings—all much-appreciated, loving, Depression gifts. At dinner one evening, Dad handed me an envelope, which I opened while my parents watched, smiling. Five ten-dollar bills, a gift from Grandpa Atlee, enough to pay my bus fare to Ontario and buy my textbooks. I had never before seen fifty dollars at one time. It seemed like a fortune and one less sacrifice for my parents.

Graduation evening. My dress was a long, bias-cut white georgette from Meier & Frank's basement. Girls carried arm bouquets of sweet peas; boys wore dark suits. We marched into the auditorium to "Pomp and Circumstance," played by the school orchestra. On the stage, I squeezed my bias-cut flounces into a chair between two sweating boys whose last names began with *B* and who were eating peanuts to show their indifference to the whole ceremony. At Grant High School, we were alphabetized to the very end.

Speeches. Awards. A walk, careful in high heels, across the stage to receive my diploma from Mr. Bittner; and in a few minutes, we were all free—free from our excellent, caring teachers who had been so concerned about their class of Depression students. I have remembered them with admiration and affection all my life—except for coaches who taught history and the gym teacher who thought I should be able to climb a rope. After the ceremony, many of us went off to drink root beer at someone's home. Gerhart avoided the whole affair.

My teeth grew straighter. Claudine invited me to Puddin' almost every weekend. It was a summer of picnics, drifting woodsmoke, laughter, splashes from the river, dancing to the piano, an accordion, or a "two-piece" orchestra. When the Canadian Legion held its picnic at the campground, the sound of bagpipes skirled through the trees while the dancers, in kilts, danced quadrilles.

When Claudine and I glimpsed stars through the leaves and fir branches, we recited

Sit, Jessica: look, how the floor of heaven
Is thick inlaid with patines of bright gold.

We had been required to recite this speech from *The Merchant of Venice* for dramatics. For me, the brightest gold in heaven was the lights of the mail plane from California coming in to land in Portland.

Mother said, "I don't think you should be spending so much time at Pudding River."

"Why not?" I asked. "Claudine and her mother invite me."

"You know why, don't you?" said Mother.

"No, why?"

"Because you keep Claudine out of Mrs. Klum's way," was Mother's strange answer. This was ridiculous, and I knew it. Claudine and her mother had a relaxed, happy relationship. I continued to accept their invitations without Mother's approval. I was braver now that escape was near.

In between weekends, Mother taught me to

338

bake a number of cakes: potato caramel cake, quick chocolate cake, Arabian spice cake, Lady Baltimore cake, prize devil's food cake, walnut loaf cake. "Always sift flour before measuring it," Mother said. "Otherwise, your cake will be heavy. Always add eggs at the last possible minute." We ate a lot of cake that summer. Mother referred to it as "Beverly's college preparatory course."

Then an outbreak of infantile paralysis spread throughout California. Mother worried. Perhaps it was not safe for me to go, after all. Dad and I ignored her worries.

Dad bought me a steamer trunk and meticulously painted my initials on the lid. I went by bus—or stage, as Grandpa called a bus—to Banks to say good-bye to my grandparents, whose store was such a social center it managed to stay in business in spite of a new chain store in Forest Grove. The customers, one after another, said to me, "You wouldn't catch me going down there to California with all those earthquakes and infantile paralysis."

Bands and wires were removed from my teeth, which were almost, but not quite, straight. Dr. Meaney said I must return to his office the next summer. (I did not. I hope I thanked him.) After six years of increasingly tight wires, my mouth suddenly felt large and roomy. My teeth no longer ached, and I smiled toothily whenever someone took a snapshot.

Gerhart resigned his job to become a Pilgrim for Jehovah's Witnesses. Prompted, I am sure, by Mother, he took me to see Leslie Howard and Bette Davis in *Of Human Bondage,* a movie I wanted very much to see and enjoyed immensely; he did not. Fu Manchu was more to his taste. As a farewell present, he gave me the box camera that had snapped pictures at the beach, on the river, and by mountain streams—pictures that often caught me in some awkward position, for this was Gerhart's sense of humor. I let him kiss me good-bye. He turned and left. I never wanted to see him again, ever. The long emotional strain had finally ended, and relief flowed through my veins.

Gerhart, three years of whose young manhood were three years of my youth—have I been fair in what I have written about him? As I look back, I can see that he was a young man who had had considerable grief and very little love in his life. He was happy to have a job, a car, and a girl. Although we spent so much time together, we understood almost nothing about each other. The difference in our ages was too great, our interests too diverse. I know that toward the end I made him very unhappy. For this I am sorry.

I should have defied Mother's manipulation of

my life, but at that time and place, parents did not tolerate rebellion from children. Gerhart, free from parents and older than I, should have let me go. We both would have been spared grief, and he would soon have found another girl, for he was a good-looking young man with a good job. And Mother—well, Mother would have found some other way to direct my life, which, in the narrow middle-class world of Portland during the Depression, had somehow become her life. She had no other interests.

My father. What did he think of this odd triangle? Even though he made an effort at conversation, his relationship with Gerhart was courteous, almost formal. Mother was right when she told me Dad did not like him, but any discussion about Gerhart took place when I was out of the house. Dad quietly observed Mother's relentless control over me, and my growing desperation. When escape was unexpectedly offered, he saw it as an opportunity, not only for a year of college, but as a way of ending my relationship with Gerhart. As I look back, I can see that my father, even though I did not ask, always understood what I wanted—roller skates, a hard sponge-rubber ball, a hemp jump rope, a bicycle, and now, freedom. I was leaving.

Because I was going so far, all the way to Southern California, friends, relatives, and neighbors came to say good-bye, to ask if I wasn't afraid of going down to California where they had all those earthquakes. Wasn't I afraid of catching infantile paralysis? Displaying my toothy new smile, I said I was not afraid. This was considered either brave or foolhardy, depending on who was doing the considering.

Mother served ice cream and slices of my college preparatory course to every visitor. Everyone was hopeful about the future. Some of President Roosevelt's programs just might help, you never could tell. If Social Security actually passed, it would be a big help in old age, that was sure. Mother felt that the end of Prohibition would not do this country one bit of good, "and I can tell you that."

Depression anecdotes were exchanged. Dad boasted that he had made one razor blade last an entire year by sharpening it on the inside of a straight-sided glass. Other men said they would try it, too. Friends laughed with Mother about her lavish use of almond extract. Mrs. Klum told of her struggles and failures in learning to knit up runs in silk stockings with a crochet hook. Mrs. Miles confided that oil discovered under her mother's house in Oklahoma City had been extracted and entitled the heirs to a small royalty; along with the homestead, it was helping to carry her family through hard times. Oil! We were im-

342

pressed, and the mystery of how Mrs. Miles managed with five daughters was solved. With hope, we could laugh, even though the end of the Depression was not in sight. We were all in it together.

Departure day. My trunk was packed and sent to the Greyhound depot. My father gave me a five-dollar bill to roll in my stocking in case I lost my purse, something I would never allow to happen. My purse held, at last, a tube of lipstick. We reached the Greyhound station by bus and streetcar, talked nervously about nothing at all until my bus was called. My father kissed me good-bye; my mother did not. I boarded and found a seat on the station side where I looked down on my parents standing together, seeming so sad and lonely. We waved without smiling. We could not smile, any of us.

As the bus pulled out of the station, I looked back, filled with sorrow, as if I were standing aside studying the three of us: my gentle, intelligent father who had surrendered his heritage to support us by long days confined in the basement of a bank; my often heroic mother with her lively mind and no outlet for her energies other than her only daughter; myself, happy, excited, frightened, and at the same time filled with guilt because I was leaving my parents behind.

Somehow, I felt, I should have made Mother happy. I ached to love and be loved by her.

The bus turned the corner; I faced front toward California. The bus rumbled along through the Willamette Valley, on, on into the night, carrying me toward my future.